Sheep Tracks

Biblical Insights From A Sheepherder

Dennis Rowan

Copyright © 2006 by Dennis Rowan

Sheep Tracks
by Dennis Rowan

Printed in the United States of America

ISBN 1-59781-856-9

All rights reserved solely by the author. The author guarantees all contents are original and do not infringe upon the legal rights of any other person or work. No part of this book may be reproduced in any form without the permission of the author. The views expressed in this book are not necessarily those of the publisher.

Unless otherwise indicated, all Scripture quotations were taken from The New International Version, NIV. Copyright 1973, 1978, 1984 by the International Bible Society, published by The Zondervan Corporation. The "NIV" and "New International Version" trademarks are registered in the United States Patent and Trademark Office by International Bible Society.

Scripture references with "KJV" are from The King James Version of the Bible.

Photos within the manuscript and front cover were taken by Dennis Rowan www.HisSheepTracks.com and www.psalm23camp.com

The Front cover design was by Mark Rowan, www.foundsheep.com and www.Rowde.com

www.xulonpress.com

To My Family

my parents, Claude and Lola, who gave me guidance with freedom

my wife, Glenda, for her unconditional love

our children, their spouses and our children's children who bring us joy beyond measure

son, Michael Lloyd and wife Kitty
their daughters Sidney and Lia

son, Scott Rowan and wife, Tammy

daughter, Michelle Lloyd Miller and husband Joel
their children Jewel, Levi, Asa, and Sky

daughter, Meredith Lloyd Taitano and husband Dave
their sons Mitchell and Derek

son, Mark Rowan and wife Jenny
their daughter Elena Kay

Table of Contents

Acknowledgements xv

Introduction xvii

1. Green Pasture **23**
Sheep are creatures of habit and desire to graze near water, salt, and the comfort of shade trees, but this behavior can be very destructive and unproductive. Are people any different?

2. Mother Up – Father Up **27**
A newborn lamb needs ample time to bond with its mother. What about the born again Christian?

3. Over **31**
Persistence and patience was necessary to train my eight-year old son to train a dog an important command that would be valuable for herding our flock of sheep. How different is it to train others for discipleship to the Lord Jesus Christ?

4. Jesus and the Sheep Dog...35
You might have seen my sheep dog work, but without a daily walk with him you have no idea of what he is really like. Jesus is that way.

5. Keds and Kids 37
God removed a destructive parasite from my sheep flock after the prayer of one lady. What else will God do through our prayers?

6. Yearlings...41
Yearling sheep can be the most frustrating sheep a shepherd owns; yet they are the most valuable sheep on the farm. Young people, especially teens, have a comparable role, a challenge for parents but a valuable human resource for the future.

7. Obedience Training...45
Training our Border Collie sheep-herding dogs has shown me some things regarding our relationship to our Lord, particularly the importance of obedience.

8. End of an Era – Eggs, $80 per Dozen..........................49
It was time to take action once our chickens quit laying eggs. Do churches ever enter a molt like chickens do?

9. Sheep That Don't Flock...53
An important aspect of sheep management is to have a group of sheep that flock, or stay together as a group. This has important implications in our Christian life.

10. The Very Best Pasture..59
There are reasons why my lambs get my very best pasture. Do adult Christians do the same for their children?

11. Table in the Presence of the Enemy 63
I prepared everything my sheep needed should the enemy come, but when the enemy came the sheep literally were gone with the wind. Do Christians sometimes follow this pattern?

12. Three Strands of Wire 67
Three strands of wire to control sheep will just train them to jump through fences. Are there parallels in our Christian life; do poor standards and unclear boundaries have an adverse effect on us?

13. An Excellent Sheep Dog Doesn't Chase Rabbits 71
Christians are called to be prepared in season and out of season. King, my sheep-herding dog is an excellent example of a servant who is always ready.

14. PTL Principles for Shepherds in Training 75
My thirteen year-old son, my sheep and my sheep-herding dogs taught me something about training others.

15. My Sheep Know My Voice 79
My sheep do know my voice, but they do not always come when I call. There is a parallel between sheep and people as to why they only come at certain times.

16. What Do You Do With A Fat Sheep? 83
Fat sheep at the end of summer grazing season are usually those who failed to produce a lamb. Do we have fat Christians?

17. Until the Soil Warms 87
Waiting and watching for new seedlings to appear in my pasture taught me a lesson about patience.

18. Shepherd at the Gate 91
I had an interesting experience with a lost sheep one day. It illustrated clearly the difference between the broad road and the narrow gate and the ultimate consequence of a wrong choice.

19. Conditions are Right for What Grows There 97
Be they good grasses or bad weeds the plants found in a pasture field reflect the conditions for growth of the same. We should make careful analysis of the conditions that grow cultural trends. What conditions do we Christians provide?

20. Night Watch 101
A night watch with my sheep is tough, but sometimes necessary. Are Christians called to take the night watch?

21. Front Feet Bound, Lying on Her Side 107
I saved the life of a young healthy sheep that was entangled in a fence. That experience gave me insight as to the condition of America.

22. Each Dog Doing His Own Thing 109
One day while working with three Border Collies giving separate directions to each I received clear insight as to why Christians and/or church groups do not work together very well.

23. Hey Shepherd, Do You Smell Like a Sheep? 115
Sheep require a lot of care, and in crisis situations I have spent more time with them. The more time I spend with my sheep the more I smell like sheep. Some pastors may find themselves out of touch when they fail to spend enough time with their sheep.

24. How High's The Water Momma? 119
When water is abundant we tend to take it for granted. What about the Gospel message in America?

25. The Lead Sheep 123
Lead sheep are those who quickly go ahead of other sheep. If that lead sheep follows the shepherd, then all is well. However, if they go the wrong direction then other sheep are lead astray. This has important implications for Christian leaders.

26. To Please The Master 127
My dog King was a marvelous example of one who made every effort to please his master. I observed a young lady in her dying days make every effort to please The Master.

27. Steady on – Sit – Come by 131
King is an excellent herding dog, but at times he uses his own will to direct my sheep. These tendencies to direct the paths of my sheep according to his will is a type and shadow of how some Christian leaders direct their flocks.

28. Beyond the Breadbasket 135
My experience in agriculture revealed that although America is the breadbasket of the world, we are not feeding the world. In a like manner Christianity in America falls short in meeting the world's needs.

29. Sheep Following Sheep – Through the Fog 141
Watching my sheep one foggy morning gave me insight into reasons why Christians are allowing our culture to influence us through corrupt leaders.

30. The Other Side of the Fence **145**
Green grass on the other side of the fence is just part of the reason sheep go through fences. Man has similar challenges.

31. One Lame Sheep after Another **149**
I learned a lesson the hard way with my lame sheep. Christians in America may be doing the same.

32. Yearlings Unattended and The Second Reading of the Law **155**
Yearling sheep are very valuable, but proper training is essential. Ignorance of God's Word is a serious problem for people.

33. The Best Tasting Water in the World **159**
The spring water on our farm is great but does not compare to "the spring of the water of life."

34. Feeding and Protecting Our Lambs **161**
Lambs need more care than adult sheep. Our children are no different; parents need to provide the correct environment for them.

35. Clean Pasture **165**
Uncontaminated pasture is a must for raising lambs. What about our school-aged children?

36. Closed Herd **169**
My sheep flock made the most progress when I reduced outside influences. Christians need this model.

37. A New Working Chute 173
Changing my working chute had some risk, but good results followed. Are some church congregations afraid to make changes?

38. Under-shepherd Gets Kicked in the Head 177
When my dog was kicked by a donkey I gained insight as to what Christians should do post 9/11/91.

39. Following an Empty Bucket 179
Why would sheep run past a valuable, good tasting feed to follow an empty bucket? There is a parallel with people.

40. Taming the Coyotes 181
A change in management was necessary once coyotes moved into our area. It is analogous to government run schools.

41. Paths of Righteousness for His Name Sake 185
Sheep that frequently go through fences into a neighbor's pasture are a reflection upon the name of their shepherd. In a like matter the namesake of Jesus is reflected in our behavior.

42. Culling the Green Heads 189
Sometimes unruly sheep in my flock must be sold to prevent them from leading others astray. Are there not parallel situations for us, especially when we consider who influences our children?

43. My Sheep 193
My sheep know who I am, but they don't really know me very well because we do not have a personal relationship like the sheep in biblical times. What does this mean?

44. Good Dogs and Other Dogs...............197
My sheep-herding Border Collies and my Great Pyrenees guard dogs are valuable, but the wrong kind of dogs on our farm can spell disaster. It is no different for those who teach our children.

45. Through the Working Chute..............................201
Group dynamics is important in herding sheep. Christianity is similar, but one on one, we all must face Jesus.

46. Concluding Track - Will You Choose Pasture or Barn Lambing? 205
A crisis situation in my sheep flock challenges my flock management. The church faces the same challenge.

Acknowledgements

I am grateful to my wife Glenda, for her proof reading, her editing suggestions, and especially for her prayers for me, our children and their families.

My thanks also go to our son Mark for designing the book cover and for his photo editing work.

Introduction

This book began in July 1986 when I wrote an article called "Green Pasture" for the first issue of a newsletter named *Sheep Tracks*. The newsletter was part of a camp ministry that my wife Glenda and I started in 1985. Psalm 23 Camp gets its name from the fact that we raise sheep on our family farm. Glenda and I were not trying to start a camp; we were just trying to do something for local boys and girls.

Neither was I attempting to write a book in 1986. I was just putting on paper what I saw in our Christian culture with respect to an example with my sheep flock. For a period of twenty years I have literally observed the sheep tracks on our farm and written many short essays or articles. Many of these are contained in this book.

Those two paragraphs above are, however, a bit simplistic as an introduction of what you are about to read. My other life experiences influenced what you read here. I trusted the Holy Spirit to reveal to me through the Scriptures, through my observations of the sheep and my other life experiences.

More specifically, I spent more than 40 years directly associated with public education before that first writing in 1986. That public education experience was obtained in four different states, and in the roles of student, teacher, and school board member. I also spent many years in youth organizations during the time I was growing up on the farm. Our summer camp program has also given me opportunities to learn much about our young people. Therefore, school, church and cultural influences on our children are a major focus of much of the material written in this book.

    I accepted Jesus as my Savior when I was eight years old, the same year Dad gave me my first sheep. I grew to love the farm and particularly the animals. Although we had sheep when I was growing up, our dairy herd was the main farm enterprise. I became very active in 4-H and FFA, spending many hours at activities associated with those organizations. In retrospect, I have concluded that there are many merits to those youth organizations, but for me personally, as a Christian, I now believe there was not enough focus on the needs of others because of the excessive amount of time I spent concentrating on my own accomplishments.

    That mentality, focusing on my own abilities and accomplishments, carried over into the many years I studied the animal sciences. I obtained three college degrees prior to my employment as a college professor. One of the best moves I ever made was the decision to give up the university teaching profession in the state of Missouri 11 years after I began. I was not happy working for the government. I had seen enough (too much, to be exact) after many years attending and teaching in government run institutions.

    I just wanted to have a job where God could be boss. I decided to return to the family farm and raise sheep. This period of my life also coincided with my discovery of the truth that lies in the Word of God. My many years of formal education could be described as "books, books everywhere and not a Word to read." The move to the family farm in West Virginia to raise sheep and allowing God to be boss brought a whole new meaning to life and an unexpected focus and study of Christianity, particularly in America. It is accurate to say that my formal education added much head knowledge to my understanding of the anatomy, physiology, health and production of sheep, but it was the Bible, with my new vocation and my new attitude that revealed what I shall call God's "heart knowledge" about sheep, shepherds, man and the Good Shepherd.

Sheep-herding dogs have been a part of our sheep enterprise for about 20 years. We have had a total of five Border Collies that have provided valuable assistance with our sheep production unit, and they have also been the subject of much of the writing you find in this book. Typically, I refer to the Border Collies as my under-shepherds, and there are important implications with respect to training, obedience, and faithfulness. The examples here should help the reader understand his relationship to his Master, and the responsibility to those who depend on you for leadership.

A few years ago we obtained two Great Pyrenees dogs to guard our sheep flock. Since coyotes have gradually become a problem, we acquired these dogs to become a part of our sheep flock management. There is some limited reference to these dogs in the book.

Since the book is a collection of 46 articles over a 20-year period, I thought a chronological arrangement would be best. Although some chapters are a reflection of the period of time when they were written, the basic message remains remarkably current. As the Bible says, "There is nothing new under the sun." (Ecclesiastes 1:9)

This paragraph was added a few days after I had completed the text of this book. (or, so I thought) A crises with the sheep flock precipitated the writing of another chapter. (No. 46) I had another surprise after writing that piece. A review showed me that there was remarkable similarity of the Scriptures and the messages between the first and the last chapters of the book. I had no such plans, and I sincerely believe it was a work of the Holy Spirit to bring some things into sharp focus.

If there is a single Bible verse that tends to be a thread throughout this book, it is Isaiah 53:6, "We all, like sheep, have gone astray." If there is one underlying implication from this writer, it is that we Christians need to be proactive. We need to do something besides warm a church pew to correct some of the ways we have gone astray in America, particularly as we train our children.

While you may wish to read the articles in the order written, each chapter is a complete message. In fact, some people will find helpful information in these pages as they prepare to teach and/or preach, especially when the example of sheep is an important part of that message.

I now insert one bit of trivia into this introduction. I often admire nice photos on Christian publications only to find they usually have no direct link to what is written inside. We've done something about that here. The two photos in this introduction, plus the cover photo, were taken here at our family farm/Psalm 23 Camp. I took the photos and our son Mark did some photo editing and he designed the cover.

My cups runs over, and I pray yours does too.

Dennis Rowan
Shepherd In Training

1

Green Pasture

Therefore go and make disciples of all nations, baptizing them in the name of the Father, and of the Son, and of the Holy Spirit. (Matthew 28:19)

Summer 1986. The 1985 growing season here at Psalm 23 Camp was a great one for green pastures. We had a long grazing season with abundant pasture and hay – the best since we returned to the home farm in May 1982. Green pastures are a delight to the shepherd as well as his flock. Few things equal the pleasure of letting my sheep into a pasture that has lush green growth. Anytime I walk through a pasture, and my sheep sense that I am about to open the gate to let them enter a green pasture, there is little that will stir their interest more as they come running and bleating toward the gate.

I must add that rotating sheep frequently to new pastures is a good soil and water conservation practice, and it provides the sheep with an excellent source of feed. The sheep can quickly obtain nourishment and spend more time lying quietly in the pasture. Without this type pasture the sheep must spend many hours daily in search of food, and each is continually in competition with other sheep for what little grass there is, plus they ingest large numbers of destructive parasites.

Jesus must surely be delighted to see members of His flock that are eager to come running to the gateway that leads to the green pastures He has for us. He will certainly lead us to green pastures if we will but follow.

You might ask, "Why not open all gates on the farm or ranch and let the sheep find all the green grass?" Nice thought, but it does not work well because given their own will the sheep pick favorite grazing spots such as areas near water, shade, and salt. Then they overgraze these areas. This will eventually bring destruction to the land as well as the sheep. This happens as the sheep become parasite infested and the overgrazed land looses life-giving topsoil from erosion. Furthermore the ungrazed areas become a wasted resource; the land grows up in tall grass and woody plants (brush) that no longer convert plants into food and fiber for man.

If you and I try to graze without guidance from the Good Shepherd, we will bring destruction to ourselves and to others who we lead astray. Furthermore we will waste God's resources. Would you rather graze near the shade (that comfortable pew located in an air-conditioned building), salt (that inspirational message your pastor gives each Sunday), and water (the fellowship with friends each week); or, would you answer the call of Jesus when He said, "Therefore go and make disciples of all nations, baptizing them in the name of the Father, and of the Son, and of the Holy Spirit." (Matt. 28:19)

Be assured, I am not condemning comfortable church buildings, Christian fellowship, and good preachin' when put in proper perspective. Some of the best grassland we have here at Psalm 23 is near water and shade. However, I plan to put some temporary electric fence around one magnificent sugar maple tree that has a stream nearby. At times last summer I saw more than two hundred sheep under the shade of that one tree. They not only damaged the grass under the tree and deposited the valuable fertilizer where it will not be used; they over grazed the grass near the tree, and failed to harvest the distant pasture. Consider these facts; less than two percent of Christians' income is given to Christian causes, and of the total given only one-half percent goes to global missions. It's obvious that professing Christians spend too much time around the watering hole and favorite shade tree.

2

Mother Up – Father Up

He tends his flock like a shepherd: He gathers the lambs in his arms and carries them close to his heart; he gently leads those that have young. (Isaiah. 40:11)

October 1986. Any shepherd can tell you what mothering up means, and how important this characteristic is to the newborn lamb. The first few hours and days to the newborn are critical times. It's a time when the lamb and its mother (the ewe) get to know each other well. They must remain close to each other to form a strong bond. Should the lamb wander aimlessly away it can hinder the chances of forming a lasting bond between mother and lamb. The lamb that strays away may fall prey to some predator such as a fox or coyote that will immediately devour him.

Lamb "stealing" is common during this time of bonding or mothering up. A ewe near parturition, or birthing, will often exhibit mothering instincts that will cause her to claim the newborn of some other ewe. This is critical because the lamb has not bonded strongly with its own mother and is receptive to the mothering influences of any ewe that is willing to give it some attention and feed it.

Communication between lamb and mother is an important factor during the mothering up process. I have observed that the better mothers constantly talk to their lambs and they're always listening closely for an answer from their lamb(s). Lambs sometimes loose the will to live because they cannot hear the mother's voice. This happens when the lamb is too far away to hear the mother's call.

The newborn lamb always comes with a healthy appetite, thirsty for life-giving milk that is provided by its mother. While the lamb is born with some energy reserve, it will not sustain life for long if it is not soon fed. If the environment is harsh because of cold temperature, the lamb will perish quickly without milk from the mother. There are several things the shepherd can do to aid in this mothering up process, but I shall only emphasize the most important. The shepherd can assist with this mothering up process best by confining the ewe and her lamb in a lambing jug (pen about four to six feet square) shortly after the lamb is born to keep the two close physically with a minimum of distraction. In the natural (pasture) environment the ewe will seek an isolated protective place to mother up. The shepherd should place pregnant ewes in a pasture large enough to provide such isolation for those ewes birthing lambs.

Oh, how important for the newly saved person to have a period of bonding with our heavenly Father. I have never heard the term Fathering up, but can you not see the many parallels with the mothering up process in the sheep? I've heard ministers say that the newly saved person is very receptive to "spirits" regardless of the source. They are easily influenced by the cults, the false prophets, and other works of Satan aimed at "stealing" those newborn. The new converts to Jesus Christ must be given life-giving milk (the Word) under the direction of an earthly shepherd such as a pastor or some other Christian(s) who is solidly grounded in God's Word. Constant communication between Jesus and the newborn Christian can surely take place more readily if other Christians help provide a suitable environment, a "Fathering up" place, as it were, to isolate the newborn.

The Bible says, "He tends his flock like a shepherd: He gathers the lambs in his arms and carries them close to his heart; he gently leads those that have young." (Isaiah 40:11) With the Holy Spirit living within Christians we should do likewise to aid in the Fathering up process of the newborn in Christ.

3

Over

Train a child in the way he should go, and when he is old he will not turn from it. (Proverbs 22:6)

April 1987. It was a cold morning. Riding a tractor with no cab had the effect of lowering the wind chill factor. This daily ride to what I call "the back side of the place" was necessary to feed part of my flock. My stock dogs are vital in that effort, because they keep the sheep away from the tractor while I roll out those bales of hay. Cold mornings present a basic challenge to complete the task quickly in order to get back to the house and "thaw out" before continuing other daily chores that are not as stressful as the cold ride to the back side of the place.

As I traveled that morning I was a bit apprehensive because I was taking King, a Border Collie we raised, who at one year of age was still in elementary school by human standards. He had some training, but was far from being seasoned. He was going with me along with our two older dogs Queenie and Dottie. His mission was simply to get some experience.

As I was passing through one pasture in route I turned my bundled up body and peered from my hood looking to see if all dogs were will with me. I saw King 200 yards away in an adjoining pasture. He had taken a wrong turn several hundred yards back and was now separated from us. My first thought was, "Oh no, what will I do? If I turn and go back I'll surely freeze because of the extra time involved." There King stood on the other side of the fence wanting to follow me and the other two dogs, yet he didn't know how to get to us.

I decided to try something– it was worth the try– it might work– I certainly had nothing to loose. In a loud, clear voice I shouted, "Over, King! Over!" Praise the Lord; he did it! He sailed over that fence like a seasoned professional. It's not incredible that King jumped the fence but it is important to me as to how he arrived at that point. Our 8-year old son, Mark, had trained King the command "over" meaning jump over. That's not necessarily so remarkable either. Maybe nothing is remarkable about this story, but I learned much from the experience. You see, Mark wanted to work with the dog until soon work became work– the novelty wore off. The experience tried our patience; mine, Mark's and King's too, I suppose. I was persistent with Mark to be persistent with King. I can tell you I could have trained the dog in one-third the time it took me to train the child to train the dog.

That incident occurred a full year before I wrote this story. At this writing King is still a young dog, probably a teenager by human standards. Untrained, King would be another pet that could perhaps fetch sticks and biscuits. Left alone to run completely free he would probably be a sheep-killing dog. He is now worth thousands if he were for sale. You realize, of course, he is not worth so much just because he can jump fences. He is now a very good, but not completely trained sheep-herding dog. King learned because of our persistence, and he learned by repetition. I did not train King to jump over the four-foot fence. Mark trained him to jump a three-foot hurdle in our yard, yet King responded to my command under very challenging circumstances. A valuable dog began his training by a mere child.

Recently I heard a man teaching church growth principles telling how children can win other people to Christ. A mere child can win a valuable soul to Christ through influence. Later that week I heard a minister explain how sheep are following shepherds, and sheep are following other sheep. About a week later I saw a six year old girl with microphone in hand bring tears to the eyes of people in a church congregation as she told in her own words about poverty stricken, starving children in Africa she saw the previous night on a Christian TV broadcast. Her plea for prayer was a powerful demonstration of who Christ Jesus is in the hearts of children.

There is a Good Shepherd Jesus Christ with many under-shepherds. If you are a pastor you are certainly one of these workers. But you don't have to be a pastor to work for Him. Under-shepherds have other under-shepherds. You are training someone else whether or not you are consciously aware of it.

Our dog is worth thousands. You, your children, grandchildren or any human cannot be valued with a dollar sign. Think about the elementary school age children you know. Think about where you would like them to be as teens or young adults. Are they presently receiving the proper mindset? What do they receive repeatedly? What do they hear over and over and over that enters their minds? Will they receive from you the proper instruction that will prepare them for the time of crisis when the Good Shepherd calls loudly and clearly "Over"? Or is there a chance that their mind will be exposed to several thousand hours of TV programming written and produced by those who serve a different master?

My prayer is that you first realize that you are a shepherd-in-training and second, that you realize your responsibility to those who are under-shepherds to you. We must listen to the Good Shepherd and spend much time reading His training Manual. Then we must be persistent and patient as we teach the lessons.

4

Jesus and the Sheep Dog

Then Jesus said to his disciples, 'If anyone would come after me, he must deny himself and take up his cross and follow me.' (Matthew 16:24)

April 1987. No, I don't think Jesus had a sheep dog, but I do think the two have much in common. Some of you know Jesus and some of you have seen our sheep-herding dogs, or you know your own sheep dogs.

To know and to know of (know about) are not the same. If you have seen our dogs work sheep you know something about them and their great works, but you do not know my dogs. They are impressive in demonstrations, but no attempt on my part to demonstrate their true value can ever be accomplished. The only way you could ever possibly conceive of their works, their loyalty and their companionship, is for you to day in and day out, for weeks and months and years, walk daily and witness these wondrous sheep dogs– fascinating beyond demonstration or description.

So it is with Jesus. Many have heard of Jesus, the preaching, healing and the miracles He performed. Many people believe Jesus did these things just as people know that my dogs are wonderful servants. The greatest miracle ever performed, the greatest sermon ever preached, the greatest sacrifice ever made means little to those who only know of Jesus or know about Jesus. No man can cause you to know Jesus by actions or words. You don't know the value of my sheep dogs and you don't know my Jesus either unless day in and day out, week after week, month after month, you take the daily walks with Him. Constant companionship is the only way to know man's best Friend.

5

Keds and Kids

What other nation is so great as to have their gods near them the way the Lord our God is near us whenever we pray to him. (Deuteronomy 4:7)

May 1988. This is a story about the greatest miracle I have personally experienced from beginning to end. A lot of people have heard of sheep ticks. While most people, including shepherds, often talk about sheep ticks, the correct term for this well-known external parasite is sheep ked. Keds are bloodsucking parasites that worry the sheep, drain them of their strength, and they do extensive permanent damage to the skin. They are usually found in greatest numbers during late winter and early spring. Treatment can reduce their numbers, but it is extremely difficult to completely rid all ticks from a flock of sheep.

During the spring of 1988 Patty Wade, children's pastor at New Life Church in Charleston, WV was visiting Psalm 23 Camp for the first time. During her visit here Glenda and I shared with her the problem we had each year with keds in our sheep flock. Just prior to leaving our place she offered to pray for Psalm 23 Camp, the farm, our personal lives, etc. Without hesitation Patty stated the fact she wished to pray for any problems with our flock including the ked infestation. She prayed with us and left.

Last week (about 10 months since her visit) we had 174 head of our sheep shorn. Keds are easy to see when the wool is being clipped. I personally saw every sheep being sheared. I did not see one single ked. Likewise, the young man shearing the sheep saw no keds. Do I think the prayers took care of the keds? I sure do. I have no reason to believe otherwise. My guess is that few people (professing Christians included) will be bold enough to repeat this story unless the motive is to make a joke of the matter. However, if I had some real harebrained story about how I did something different to the flock this year like turning them in to the woods to eat brush, then some would want to investigate the matter to see what actually got rid of the keds. We have a tendency to try to "explain away" what God does by saying, "Well, that just happened".

What about big-time prayers? We don't like to admit it, but from a moral standpoint the United States of America is about bankrupt. Why not put our faith out for our nation's healing. America was founded on Christian principles, but we have not maintained right standing with God.

After God had used many signs and wonders to deliver the Israelites from Egypt giving constant protection and provision he used Moses to give them this message as recorded in the fourth chapter of Deuteronomy. "What other nation is so great as to have their gods near them the way the Lord our God is near us **whenever we pray** to him." (Emphasis added.) I'll let you decide whether that message to Israel applies to America now.

Verse 9 in that message reads, "Only be careful, and watch yourselves closely so that you do not forget the things your eyes have seen or let them slip from your heart as long as you live. **Teach them to your children and to their children** after them. (Emphasis added.)

Do you see what I see in this passage of Scripture? Our Lord our God is near us whenever we pray. Would the reverse be true, the Lord is far from us when we fail to pray? We are to watch closely, remember what we see and **teach these things to our children!** I thank God for removing the keds from my flock of sheep; my kids will be taught that; and I thank God for Patty Wade because I have knowledge of what and how she teaches kids (and adults) about prayer. What about you? You may not have a problem with **keds**, but you surely have an opportunity with **kids**!

6

Yearlings

– Teach them to your children and to their children after them. (Deuteronomy 4:9)

Summer 1988. Have you ever seen yearling sheep? They're those gangly creatures that aren't cute little lambs anymore, but they're not grownups yet. As their name implies, yearlings are those sheep that are around a year old. If we were talking in human terms, a yearling would be right there in that teenager bracket. And, like their human counterparts, yearlings just aren't like anything else. In fact, the only thing predictable about yearlings is that they are always unpredictable.

Ask any shepherd about his yearlings, and chances are you'll witness the whole gamut of emotions. He'll probably tell you how the yearlings are constantly jumping the electric fences, ones that his horses wouldn't even consider jumping. He'll tell you about how they seem to have no fear of the sheep-herding dogs. I've seen some pretty puzzled expressions on the faces of my own dogs when they try to herd a bunch of yearlings.

Yearlings will look at an ear of corn lying on the ground in front of them making no attempt to eat the grain their mamas would trample one another trying to get the first bite of such a treat. And they know practically nothing about following the other sheep in an orderly fashion into the pens and corrals.

When they give birth, a mature ewe is usually grateful to the shepherd for any help he may give her through such an ordeal. She may rest quietly for a few moments before she gets up and starts talking to and licking her precious new lamb. When yearlings give birth to their first lamb it is a totally different story. Trying to help a yearling give birth to her lamb is a lot like calf roping in a rodeo. On one occasion I delivered a newborn from a yearling, and in an instant the yearling jumped up and went tearing off across a twenty-acre field like a rodeo calf out of the starting gate.

Yes, yearlings are unpredictable, ungrateful, unmanageable, and well, unlikable much of the time. But a shepherd will tell you something else about his yearlings, that they are the most valuable sheep on the farm.

Maybe they are not the best-behaved or the most productive sheep on the farm, but their value exceeds all others because of the potential they have for the future productivity of the flock. A yearling is rapidly approaching adulthood, and the success of the entire flock will rest with this sheep.

Teenagers and young adults have similar responsibilities that will soon rest upon their shoulders. And right now, they are oftentimes unpredictable, ungrateful, unmanageable, and even unlikable. And, like yearlings, they are our most valuable resource.

Yearlings are not really just a hopeless bunch of renegades; they just act like it. In fact, if the shepherd spends a little extra time with his lambs before they reach the yearling stage, they are really quite nice to work around. The problem is that most shepherds just don't take the extra time that is necessary and crucial to build a relationship with the young sheep. But how else are they supposed to develop trust in the shepherd?

The same is true for our kids. Christian adults are more likely to help the young become more productive in the Lord's work if they'll spend the extra time and effort. Unfortunately, our churches are often in reverse; we spend more time, effort and money feeding ourselves than we do feeding and caring for the young. Furthermore, all the time children spend away from home in school classrooms takes time away from parents who are the primary shepherds of those young lambs.

7

Obedience Training

If you love me, you will obey what I command. (John 14:15)

November 1988. The sheep dogs at Psalm 23 camp are invaluable. Nothing can replace them. No man has the swiftness of a Border Collie. You and I may be able to think quickly and determine what needs to be done in an emergency with respect to a group of sheep, but we cannot complete most of the tasks the dogs do in such an effortless fashion. I've never seen a dog show and never taken dogs to a dog obedience school. I have been privileged to talk to trainers of Border Collies, read books, and I have trained dogs, not for show or dog field trials, but for the day to day practical sheep flock management.

Our dogs are capable of learning dozens of commands. They learn quickly and they love to please their master. They do, however, have some faults that often reflect characteristics of people, people like you and me.

Although our dogs know many commands, less than a dozen are necessary for the hard-core sheep handling details here at Psalm 23. Dog trainers can teach dogs a lot of cute little things that amuse us and this has some value for entertainment and for demonstrating what dogs are capable of learning. You can see that at a circus. Unfortunately there are times around here that it appears as though we are part of a circus, complete with any clowns that might be found in the area, but we do not plan it that way. On the contrary, our dogs work very hard most of the time and cuteness is not our objective.

Dogs have what I call different levels of learning and obedience. The first level comes when a dog responds to my command while still on a twelve-foot training leash. If the dog disobeys I still have control with the leash. From that the dog graduates to the second level, which is obedience to commands without the restrictions of a leash. If he becomes disobedient then we go back to step one until the lesson is learned.

Level-three obedience is the dog's response to commands under moderate stress, pressure, or distraction. You see it's one thing for a young dog to obey without hesitation in a relaxed environment with no other animals or people around to turn the dog's attention away from my commands, but it's something else to obey with multiple distractions.

Level-four obedience is response under heavy pressure, during a crisis or emergency. It can be described in the framework of "Dog, do it now, this ain't no puppy dog training session!" One distinct difference between level four and the first three levels is that disobedience at level four does not call for reprimand and/or retraining. You see, the dog may get reprimanded for being disobedient followed by retraining in levels one, two, and three to make sure the lesson is learned. At level three a dog may take a short cut because of laziness. If that goes uncorrected it will be easier for the same disobedience the next time that temptation comes. Reprimand is necessary, but retraining may not be. In many cases, I know, and the dog knows he has been disobedient. I may give a command; the dog disobeys, and followed by my loud voice that says only the dog's name. The firmness in my voice causes the dog to finally obey. Many people have experienced the same thing with their children.

You might say school is not in session when we operate at obedience level number four. School is out; we are not teaching that lesson any more. It is time for serious business. I know what needs to be done and I give the command, for example, for my dog to circle the flock approaching them from the left side as the dog faces the sheep. To the dog this may appear exactly like a situation we had the day before at the same location. Let's say the dog disobeys, circles the opposite way, the sheep crowd against a temporary fence I just put up this morning. Then they crash through the fence, become entangled in it, and then mix with another group of sheep. We have a situation where the obedient dog within 30 seconds could have corralled the sheep and we would continue about our business. With disobedience in this example the 30 seconds could turned into destruction of the fence and perhaps another two to three hours to gather the sheep and sort them into the correct groups.

Obedience at level four means complete obedience. When I give the command the dog either does exactly as I say and when I say it or I have a disaster on my hands. An additional point is worth emphasizing; potentially disastrous situations seldom depend upon a dog's knowledge of a large number of commands. The example given above depicts a disaster that resulted from disobedience to one single command.

What about us, you and me? What about Christians and their obedience levels? What about Adam? God didn't give some elaborate list of trees and fruits with complicated directions about what to eat and what to leave alone, did He? God gave one command; "And the Lord God commanded the man' You are free to eat from any tree in the garden; but you must not eat from the tree of the knowledge of good and evil, for when you eat of it you will surely die'" (Genesis 2:16-

17). Talk about disaster for a lack of level-four obedience! What about God's command to Abraham to offer his son Isaac as a sacrifice? It was a simple command. Abraham was obedient even though he didn't understand everything God was doing. Abraham didn't need to understand anything other than God's command.

We sometimes get a command from God and then try to lean on our own understanding as how it is to work out, or more likely how it will not work. Based on our understanding we try to put God off. Or, we propose Plan B to God. God has **a** plan it is Plan A. If you and I insist on operating at obedience levels one, two and three when He calls for level-four obedience, He may quietly send us to the kennel. Are you familiar with the story of Moses and why God did not allow him to enter the Promised Land? I sometimes quietly take a disobedient dog to the kennel and then get one of the other dogs that I trust will do the job.

The Bible is full of references to man's obedience and disobedience, but I wish to call your attention to some things Jesus said about obedience as found in the 14th chapter of John. "If you love me, you will obey what I command." (vs. 15) "If anyone loves me, he will obey my teaching– " (vs. 23). "– the world must learn that I love the Father and that I do exactly what my Father has commanded me– " (vs. 31).

8

End of an Era – Eggs, $80 per Dozen

For the time will come when men will not put up with sound doctrine. Instead, to suit their own desires, they will gather around them a great number of teachers to say what their itching ears want to hear. (2 Timothy 4:3)

March 1989. The burning building collapsed under the weight of the metal roof. Earlier that morning we had made the final decision, the decision to burn a small building that was in view of our house and also in full view of my parents' home.

This building could be called a haybine shed, but then never in my life have I heard a building called a haybine shed. It did, however, house our haybine each year for about nine months when we were not cutting hay. We sometimes called it a doghouse. What is your image of a doghouse? Is it a building approximately 12 feet by 20 feet standing six feet tall. I didn't think so. Although three of our Border Collies made this their house, we somehow found it difficult to call it a doghouse. Most of the time we called it a chicken house.

The building was constructed to house chickens, but a chicken had not been near that building in nearly forty years.

When our chicken house was nearly completely burned (we were getting rid of an eyesore on the property) my Mom said with a chuckle, "Well, that's the end of an era, the chicken house is gone." Although I remember the time when we had laying hens, and generally knew why my parents quit raising them, details of the specific circumstances that existed many years ago only surfaced while Mom and Dad reminisced as the ashes cooled. My Dad recalled how he had purchased 35 laying hens that consistently laid about 33 eggs daily that first summer. According to him they "laid their eyeballs out" until they went into a molt in late summer. The molting condition consists of hormone changes that cause the birds to reduce and/or cease laying until the following spring.

The next spring the anticipated laying season never came. Dad related how he one day made the decision to switch from a hope for eggs to a reality of fried chicken. They butchered all 35 hens and put them in the freezer. (You might say a bird in the skillet is worth two or more that aren't on the nest). After eating $20 worth of feed those hens produced a total of only 3 eggs that second year – that does make egg-eating a bit expensive at $80.00 a dozen.

While most examples in the agricultural economy are not this extreme, it is something farmers have experienced over the past several decades. It seems a farm enterprise can only hope to be profitable when the farmer specializes. Therefore most farmers have a very few varieties of crops or livestock but try to increase efficiency by producing a larger quantity of the few types of products they raise. There are people who raise chickens because they enjoy feeding and caring for the chickens, there are those who raise sheep for the same reason. Like examples are found with cattle, hogs, goats, ducks, etc. These are sometimes referred to as hobby farmers or gentlemen farmers. As I think about changes in agriculture I am also reminded of some parallel changes in our churches. Sometimes our Christianity follows that pattern. It's easy to turn inward and do those things that nurture our own well being or self gratification. Here are some new terms for you, "hobby Christian" and gentleman Christian". I could give many examples of church activities that seem to have little or nothing to do with finding lost souls and winning them to the Lord Jesus Christ.

To a large extent many church congregations have become bogged down with tradition, procedural matters and placing more emphasis on what's put on paper (reporting numbers) than what's preached from the pulpit. By contrast, some are saying, "Lets simply turn outward, preach the uncompromised Word of God and win souls."

In summary, let me say that if your church has gone into a molt with a large feed bill (church budget) and you are producing very few eggs (converting lost souls to Jesus Christ), maybe your eggs are costing $80 per dozen, so to speak. If so, it might be time to try something different. If not, we may be near the end of an era. As a matter of fact, I have a strange notion that whether we change as individuals and congregations or we choose not to change, we are nevertheless on the very edge of the end of an era. Don't accept my strange notion; check your Bible and prayer closet.

9

Sheep That Don't Flock

My people have been lost sheep; their shepherds have led them astray and caused them to roam on the mountains. They wandered over mountain and hill and forgot their own resting place. Whoever found them devoured them; their enemies said, "We are not guilty, for they sinned against the Lord, their true pasture, the Lord, the hope of their fathers." (Jeremiah 50:6-7)

June 1989. The characteristic that sheep have of flocking together is very important for those of us who raise them, particularly when the number of sheep exceeds 50 or 60 head. The larger the flock the more important it is that the sheep have a strong flocking instinct. Protection from predators is a primary reason sheep stay together. In the face of danger a scattered flock of sheep in a pasture will flow together as if they were caught in a huge funnel, or as though some huge magnet near the center of the flock had suddenly been switched on.

This flocking instinct is an asset to the shepherd. With the help of our sheep dogs a flock of 300 to 400 head of sheep can be gathered and lead out of a 20 acre field in less than five minutes. A good stock dog can gather other livestock such as cattle or hogs but not as quickly as with sheep. The reason lies in the fact that sheep have a much stronger flocking instinct. Once the sheep see the dogs they flock together into a compact group that is then swiftly moved along.

Technical research trials have shown and experienced shepherds will concur that it takes four or more sheep to make a flock. Three sheep in a field with no other sheep in view cannot see an identifiable group to go join. They tend to race about in panic not knowing where to go. If only two sheep are in a field, each can obviously see only one other sheep, and thus neither one sees a group to join. One sheep in a large field cannot be driven. One cow can be driven. One hog can be driven. One sheep by itself will simply not move in any orderly fashion.

From a shepherd's management standpoint a sheep that gets separated from the flock presents a serious problem. Many times my dogs and I have gathered a flock of 200 to 300 sheep from a field in approximately 5 to 10 minutes, followed by a period of 30 to 45 minutes that the dogs and I spend getting one more sheep. In more recent years I seldom take the time to get the one that failed to flock. I leave them in the field. Let me explain why I leave them in the field. Why should I take 45 minutes with one sheep doing the same job that took five minutes with 300 sheep (one second per sheep)? Forty-five minutes per sheep versus one second per sheep is a vast difference.

This past week was particularly busy as I worked with 400 sheep that were in four different groups. These were moved to and from pasture fields two separate times to perform certain tasks in the working chute. That's 16 trips. (eight trips to the corral and eight trips back to the pastures) Now if my work was delayed for 45 minutes each of the 16 trips because of the failure of one sheep each time to follow the flock that would have been 12 extra hours of work. Can you imagine a pastor who takes three deacons (I usually use three sheep dogs) each time there is a church service and travels to someone's home, knocks on the door and helps that person get to church simply because they failed to do what the rest of the flock did?

There are two reasons that I have identified among my sheep as to why they deliberately chose to stray from the flock. One is greed. Sheep are more eager to chow down on the grass than to be concerned about joining the rest of the flock. A second reason is that some sheep just seem to have a strong will to be independent. At times while in the confines of a small field or corral there are individual sheep that bolt or break away from the flock. The interesting part is how they do this repeatedly in an almost defiant manner. In a large open pasture some seem to just wander aimlessly away from the flock for no obvious reason. Sheep that don't flock are ones who have deliberately gone astray. For purposes of explanation here I classify lost sheep as those who are separated from the flock but for reasons other than greed or a will for independence.

What's wrong with the sheep that chooses to go its own way? In some cases death is the end result. I'm reminded of the story told by my friend Joe Harper of Mouth of Seneca, WV who had a sheep that chose not to follow the flock as he was gathering them. He made the decision, as I likely would have, that the ewe would need to be left and gathered later somehow. Here's what happened. Her lamb followed her, thus another was led astray. When he returned some time later he found the carcasses that indicated a bear had devoured them both. On two separate occasions this year I had dogs attack my sheep that had strayed from the flock. Predators can pick off a stray sheep much easier, and as their shepherd I can't do much to protect them if they are not with the group of several hundred that is easy to find, particularly in mountain and hill country that is thickly covered with trees and brush.

In other cases the sheep may just miss out on the care to be given by the shepherd. It may be the green pasture, still water, restored soul, safety from the shadow of death (Joe's sheep missed this one), a table of grain, or perhaps an anointing with trichlorform, fenbendazole or some other present day treatment analogous to the oil as referred to in the twenty-third Psalm.

God's word says in Isaiah 53:6 (KJV), "We all, like sheep, have gone astray, each of us has turned to his own way –" That includes the two of us, you and me. I am sure that pastors can relate to sheep that don't flock within their congregation but my heart at this writing is burdened with the flock of sheep that I shall call citizens of America. Jeremiah 50:6-7 states it this way, "My people have been lost sheep; their shepherds have led them astray and caused them to roam on the mountains. They wandered over mountain and hill and forgot their own resting place. Whoever found them devoured them; their enemies said, 'We are not guilty, for they sinned against the Lord, their true pasture, the Lord, the hope of their fathers.'"

During the course of my lifetime I have seen greed and a will for independence cause people to roam the mountains. The "me generation" of false shepherds has substituted for the word "sin" numerous other socially accepted terms such as consenting adults, alternative lifestyles, situation ethics, pro-choice, values clarification, adult entertainment, and misappropriation of funds. We have forgotten our resting place because a declining percentage of people claim that Jesus is Lord of their life. Jesus is seldom mentioned in the work place. His name can't be used in our schools (so they say) because many believe it to be unlawful; it seems as though the only way Jesus is mentioned on the nightly news or written into movie and television scripts is in a blasphemous manner. Attitudes, philosophies, and laws have devalued the family as an important institution.

Do you think that divorce, child abuse, homosexuality, pornography, alcohol related auto fatalities, fatal drug overdoses, vandalism, suicide, crime among elected officials and occult worship have any relationship to sheep who have gone astray? Who is guilty, the enemy (Satan, the tempter), or is it the sheep who choose to wander away on their own? America was built upon Christian principles. The hope of America's forefathers seemed to have been well established. Have we forgotten that the Lord is our true pasture and in the process become sheep that don't flock? Have most Americans left the true pasture?

10

The Very Best Pasture

When they had finished eating, Jesus said to Simon Peter, 'Simon son of John, do you truly love me more than these?' 'Yes, Lord,' he said, 'you know that I love you.' Jesus said, 'Feed my lambs.' (John 21:15)

October 1989. Visitors to Psalm 23 frequently ask soon after their arrival, "Where are your sheep?" I then proceed to tell and/or show them. There is no time when all sheep are in the same pasture. There will always be at least two groups depending upon the time of year, the types of sheep, and the state of production (pregnant, non-pregnant, milking, growing, etc.).

As the lambs grow older the ewes' milk volume declines and the lambs depend more upon the pasture to meet their needs for growth. As this occurs the lambs compete with the older sheep for grass. The pastures also become more contaminated with internal parasite eggs and larvae as the season extends into mid and late summer. These factors begin to work against the lambs' health and growth.

Sometime in July or August I wean all the lambs and place them on the very best pasture available. It is often hay aftermath or re-growth. In other words, it is grass that has grown back after a crop of hay has been removed. In addition to the nutritious new growth, this land is also clean with respect to parasites because sheep have not grazed it that season. Lambs are given the best because of what they are to become, not what dollar value they have at that point.

If this weaning process takes place during winter months the shepherd formulates the very best diet for these lambs. They get the best hay and the right combination of grains.

In our Christian life we should follow the same management as shepherds; we should provide the very best pasture for the lambs. For a long time I've been intrigued about Jesus' command to Peter (John 21: 15-17). Jesus made three statements to Peter concerning feeding and caring for the sheep, and isn't it interesting that the first of these three statements was "Feed my lambs." Perhaps he meant lambs to be top priority just as shepherds do.

Does your church spend as much time, effort and money on children's programs as on the adults? Is more money invested in the children's choir or music program than on the adults? Is your youth pastor given top priority? Are facilities for the young in your church the very best? I was in a church once that had one room in the building that had very nice furniture (the kind a country boy would hesitate to sit on) that was bought and used by the ladies of the church. A couple doors down the hall the teen-agers had a room that was about as exciting as a West Virginia woodshed.

You see, we are much like the sheep. We compete with the lambs. We grab the new growth of grass and crowd out the lambs. We probably contaminate the pasture as well. Sometimes we think we are doing great things for our youth when in fact we may not be meeting their needs. We try to compete with the world. We may have the kids raise money so they can go somewhere next summer and ride a bigger roller coaster than they rode last summer. You might retort, "I can see no harm in that!" You know what? The destructive internal parasite eggs and larvae that sometimes kill my lambs cannot be seen in the pastures either. It takes a magnifying glass to see them. Some of the greenest pastures are loaded with these tiny, yet destructive parasites.

No, the truth is that young people need the same thing you and I need, the Word of God. Lambs should be fed the very same ingredients as older sheep; the ingredients are just formulated into a different diet, or put together in a different combination.

Finally at some point in time my lambs arrive to their function; never perfect, but they reach an acceptable level of maturity. Now if you're upset because of my negative reference to roller coasters just let me say that recreation can have its positive effects, but the total diet had better include sufficient training to provide spiritual growth in the lives of young people. How many high school students, for example, do you know that stand up and boldly proclaim Jesus as Lord of their lives? Now I don't mean did they at some time make a trip to an alter and fill out a card. All too often we are more impressed with the youngster who can slam dunk a basketball than whether or not they witness daily to others about our Lord Jesus Christ.

If a shepherd gives his best pasture to the lambs so they can arrive at an acceptable level of maturity then I leave you with three final questions. At what point do you expect young people to arrive at an acceptable level of Christian maturity? What is your idea of an acceptable level of Christian maturity? Do you think they need the very best pasture or will second best be good enough for young growing lambs?

11

Table in the Presence of the Enemy

You prepare a table before me in the presence of my enemies. (Psalm 23:5)

Spring 1990. Five of my most valuable sheep were set for the winter. The five sheep were rams less than a year old. Three had been selected as what I believed to be the best among approximately 150 other male lambs in my flock. The other two had come to these West Virginia hills from the flock of Rick and Kathy Haynes way out in Colorado.

Since a given ram is potentially the sire (father) of many lambs in one year they are important sheep because of their genetic influence. In fact, two years after the occasion described here one of these rams sired more than 100 lambs in one year. The fact that these rams were young with a full life ahead of them also contributed to their value.

These lambs, separated from the rest of the flock, were set for the winter because I had made special provision for them like I had never made for a group of sheep before. I placed them in a field near the house where I could see them daily and I kept several days feed supply (large round hay bale) before them at all times. Not more than 100 feet from the hay was a stream to provide all the fresh water they needed. They were free to eat, drink, lie down, or walk around, as they desired. As their shepherd I had "prepared a table for them" much as the Psalmist David describes in Psalm 23. Yes, you could say these sheep were set for the winter– except for one thing– the enemy.

The enemy came in mid-January 1986– a winter storm. The snow came, the temperature dropped and the winds blew. The snow piled so deep I could barely walk through it. I inspected the area where I kept the young rams and found that the table was still set; plenty of hay was available and the water supply was the same as ever, but the rams were gone– they had literally gone with the wind. Knowing sheep as I do, I was not surprised to see them gone because they do tend to follow the wind during a storm. Quite frankly, I knew that was a part of their provision that I knew had a fault. You see, their "table" was in one corner of a very large field and it was adjacent to the mountain where sheep could literally travel for miles.

The rams were gone and the snow was blowing so badly and piled so deep that any attempt to find them would have been foolish and dangerous. I would not be able to find tracks and white sheep don't show up well in snow. Three days later I discovered all five young rams with the rest of the flock approximately one-half mile away. I can tell you it was a happy ending to a potentially disastrous situation.

Think about it; the sheep had everything they needed, the storm came and they were driven from their secure place. They had no reason to leave the storm with all their provision right in front of them. Does that describe how we Christians act at times? We have accepted Jesus Christ as Savior and Lord, but when the storms in life come with chilling gusty winds do we not leave the table at times? The experience with my sheep was but another example of how people and sheep are so much alike, but we can take comfort in knowing God is always there to help us. I couldn't follow my sheep in the storm, but God will always be with you should a storm come your way.

12

Three Strands of Wire

Folly is bound up in the heart of a child, but the rod of discipline will drive it far from him. (Proverbs 22:15)

June 1990. Several years ago I built a semi-permanent electric fence with three strands of wire. Three years later I tore it completely down and replaced it with better materials. More importantly I constructed it using five strands of wire. We now have on the farm, high tensile strands of wire on fences that are either four or five strands. A single strand can contain most horses, two or three can do a reasonable job with cattle, but sheep need at least five.

Three strands of wire for sheep is worse than no fence at all. Oh, you can with proper management contain sheep for a while with three strands, but in the long run a fence constructed with three strands of wire merely **trains the sheep to jump through fences.**

Once the sheep learn they can easily penetrate the three strands of wire then the fence is useless. What is worse is the fact that the sheep then makes no distinction between three, four, or even five strands; they charge through all of them.

The pulsating electric charge is not enough to deter a fast moving sheep with a coat of wool.

So it is in the life of man. Put God's standards aside, construct your own three-stranded wire fence and before long there is chaos. Letting children make important decisions too early in life is a three-stranded fence. I recently heard someone describe a PG (Parental Guidance) rated movie by saying it was **not too bad**. My three strands of wire were not too bad for a while. How does this sound to you; "It was **not too ungodly.**"? How should a parent view a PG movie? He shouldn't. I use to be a little confused about what PG meant in the movie industry. I asked myself the question, "Does that mean I must view the film first to determine if it is suitable for children?" Or, do I simply decide if my child is mature enough to watch the film? We are still dealing with three strands of wire. If someone has put a Parental Guidance rating on a movie it means there is questionable material in the movie. If it is questionable, neither I nor my children need to view it. Children who watch PG movies are being trained to jump through the fences, pure and simple.

Several years ago I met what I considered to be a very spiritual married couple that was very active in their local church. I was shocked to learn that they had a teen-ager who chose not to attend church with them. Sadly, I have found that to be true with many churchgoers. In other cases parents may require their children to attend Sunday morning services, but let the children decide if they want to attend other activities such as youth meetings. We get down to about one or two strands of wire when we let young children decide whether or not they will accompany their parents to church.

I have learned from Christian School administrators that it is not uncommon for Christian parents to let their children decide whether they attend a secular or Christian school. I question the wisdom of telling a child he must do certain things like go to the doctor or dentist, but when it comes to matters of Christianity, then the child is placed on his own to decide. Three strands of wire won't hold my sheep, and they won't hold our children. For that matter, three strands of wire won't hold you and me either.

For me personally, one of the most difficult areas of my life is putting up and keeping the fourth and fifth strands of wire that relate to daily Bible study and prayer. I know it is the correct thing to do, but the "cares of this world" have a way of tearing down those extra strands. Check these statistics for the value of a fence that keeps you in the right pasture: divorce rate for Christians who attend church together is one out of 50 while the divorce rate among all Americans is one out of two. The divorce rate for Christians who attend church and also pray together regularly is one out of over 1150. (Source: *What God Hath Joined*, by Robert Paul Lamb, Eternal word Publishing, 1989) You will not hear that statistic on the six o'clock news or read it in a school textbook. **Does prayer build fence?**

From the guidance we give young people in their formative years to the self-discipline we develop ourselves, it is imperative that well-defined boundaries surpass the three-stranded variety I had for my sheep. However, we do need to realize that strict legalism based on man-made rules can also fall short. Jesus said it this way, "Woe to you, teachers of the law and Pharisees, you hypocrites! You clean the outside of the cup and dish, but inside they are full of greed and self-indulgence. (Matt. 23:25)

13

An Excellent Sheep Dog Doesn't Chase Rabbits

Preach the Word; be prepared in season and out of season; correct, rebuke and encourage– with great patience and careful instruction. For the time will come when men will not put up with sound doctrine. Instead, to suit their own desires, they will gather around them a great number of teachers to say what their itching ears want to hear. They will turn their ears away from the truth and turn aside to myths. (2 Timothy 4:2-4)

Winter 1990. Not more than fifteen feet from were we walked a Cottontail rabbit jumped up and ran directly in front of us. I was startled; the rabbit did not startle me, but the behavior of my companion did. King, a five-year old, faithful Border Collie sheep dog merely turned his head to watch the rabbit rapidly run by us. King did not seem to flex a single muscle that would indicate a desire to chase that rabbit. That, in essence, is what surprised me so, the fact that King made no effort to chase the rabbit. I was so startled because I had never seen a dog remain so calm while a rabbit jumped and ran like that. During my lifetime I have seen similar circumstances many times with other dogs, and in all such cases the dog, or dogs with me have always made a mad dash to chase the rabbit.

I doubt if thirty seconds had passed after that incident before I realized why King did not chase the rabbit. King was trained to be a sheep-herding dog. He is well disciplined, loyal, and has always been under my direction when he is working. He has had little time to roam the farm on his own. King is kept in a kennel when he is not working or in fellowship with one of the members of our family. King is an excellent sheep dog. We have two other fully trained sheep dogs that are very good. People who have seen Queenie and Dottie work may call them excellent sheep dogs. However, Queenie and Dottie chase rabbits. These two dogs were fully trained when we bought them. The previous owners had taught them well with respect to herding sheep, and with respect to hunting groundhogs and a doing a number of other things. They are excellent in many ways, but compared to King, they must receive a lower rating. They are very good while he is excellent.

When I release my dogs from the kennel to walk across the farm I often tend to miscellaneous chores before, in between, and after herding sheep. At such time that I am ready to do serious business herding sheep I naturally look to these dogs for assistance. The excellent dog is at my side and ready for my commands. I often have some trouble getting an exact location on the other two dogs because they like to go on their own hunting for groundhogs, rabbits, or some other animal. Don't you know I prefer to work with a dog that is ready to work when the work is ready?

When Paul wrote his second letter to Timothy he told him to "– be prepared in season and out of season–" (2 Tim 4:2), and you and I both know Paul was not talking about rabbit season. The Bible makes a lot of reference to taking care of sheep, but as far as I know God has nowhere in His Word instructed us to chase rabbits. But on the other hand I have a feeling that Christians, for a period of nearly two thousand years, have been chasing a lot of rabbits. A sheep dog should be trained to herd sheep and nothing more. Unlike King, the two sheep dogs that chase rabbits fail to be prepared to herd sheep at all times. In many instances Christians literally let the rabbit "wag" the dog. Chasing rabbits may seem like a harmless activity, but it prevents the dog from being prepared at all times to herd sheep. Furthermore we must realize that hunting is for hound dogs.

Christians get involved in all manner of rabbit chasing. Sometimes it is a successful program that draws crowds, but builds on sand rather than rock. Some churches have chased rabbits so far that they finally leave the sheep pasture and reach the dense thickets of brush and briers – the place in which rabbits love to dwell, but the sheep seldom visit. Someone recently told me what a disgrace they thought it was that a major main line denominational church in America brought to vote year after year the issue as to whether or not homosexuals should be ordained as ministers in that denomination. Those type issues are not brought to vote in a sheep pasture. That's a brier patch issue.

But then a lot of rabbit chasing is still of the sheep pasture variety – the type things that are more subtle and generally accepted by many Bible believing Christians. For example, quilt making, Christmas crafts, the ladies' group, the men's group, the roller-skating, and many other social activities that lead people out of hearing distance of the Shepherd. Some things, like Christian rock music may be good for getting some lost young people saved, but do little to train the saved to become disciples. A puppy is loved, protected, placed in a kennel and given care, but the day comes when he must learn to herd sheep according to the master's teaching.

Let's look at 2 Tim 4:2-4, with my remarks in parentheses. "– I give you this charge: Preach the Word; be prepared in season and out of season; correct (sheep dogs need it), rebuke (sheep dogs need it) and encourage (sheep dogs need it) – with great patience (the shepherd needs it) and careful instruction (the sheep dogs need it). For the time will come when (the rabbit season opens) men will not put up with sound doctrine (principles of sheep herding). Instead, to suit their own desires (to chase anything that moves), they will gather around them a great number of teachers (hound dogs; you also get fleas when you run with hounds) to say what their itching ears want to hear (sic 'em). They will turn their ears away from the truth (Bible) and turn aside to myths. (chasing rabbits)

14

PTL Principles for Shepherds in Training

A wise son heeds his father's instruction – (Proverbs 13:1)

January 1991. For approximately nine years sheep and shepherds have been on the hillsides here at Psalm 23 Camp, even though the camp ministry has been in existence for less than six years, at this writing. The shepherds have and presently consist of my family and me. For seven of those nine years Border Collie sheep dogs have been a significant part of the sheep operation that consists of more than 500 head of sheep most months of the year.

Herding sheep is not easy. When we had less than 100 sheep the family could do a reasonable job, but with 500 the dogs are a necessity. Dogs can function under only one master at a time. Authority can be transferred from me to another family member if I am not present. Even then the new master must gain the confidence of the dog, and a firm rule must be exercised.

As our son Mark grew from a six year old to his thirteenth year the dogs gained his confidence as a playmate and caretaker (he fed and watered them). However, Mark was limited to working with only one of the three dogs. The other two dogs would not be obedient; they did not view him as their master, one with the authority to command them. It became an accepted fact that I was the only person who could handle all three dogs. This severely restricted the sheep operation because all dogs don't perform all tasks equally well.

Then in the summer of Mark's thirteenth year I became so busy I knew we needed to try some new approaches, plus I sensed that he was actually old enough to handle all the dogs. As a result, Mark was easily working any one of the dogs by midsummer. He could literally be sent any place on the farm with even the toughest handling dog and get the job done of assisting me with sheep herding details.

This new approach was operating successfully for a few weeks before I analyzed it and discovered the PTL principles. These principles can work in any other leadership training situations as well as it does with herding sheep. What is PTL? One day I was thinking, "What did we really do to make this work?" I began to think about what I had done consistently that summer as I sent Mark to herd sheep.

There are a lot of hazards in herding sheep with dogs. Sheep can be harassed, scattered, injured, and lost. Fences can be torn down and general chaos can permeate the entire place including sheep, dogs, and family. I always prayed over these situations as I released Mark to the task at hand.

I also put my trust in Mark believing he would be sincere in his efforts. I put trust in God that the entire situation would be under His care. I knew mistakes would be made. I knew it would be a learning situation for Mark and the sheep dogs. Even the sheep would need to gain confidence in Mark as a shepherd. Part of the element of trust hinged on the belief that long-range gains would out weigh short-term problems.

One day I gave Mark an assignment to go get a group of sheep and move them across the farm to another location. I then went about some other chore. From where I was working I could see Mark at a distance of about one-fourth mile away. I could tell by the behavior of the sheep which dog Mark had chosen to work with that day. I could see there were potential problems, but I had already put confidence in the basic idea that it was better that I trust Mark to learn certain things by experience rather than give him some great long list of do's, don'ts, ifs, etc. It was comforting to me to learn from him later how he had certain problems and learned appropriate remedies as he voluntarily told me what had happened that day.

In addition to the prayer before giving Mark a task, and the trust that I released, I also did a third thing; I let go. Is there a difference between trust and let go?

For my definition, trust means I believe that someone can do the same job I do, even though I know I can do it better (this is often a false assumption). I think I can do a job at 100% while the person I trust with the job can only come to 65%. The 65% level is good enough, especially for the one who is just learning. Given enough time the other person may perform at the 125% level compared to me; maybe 150, maybe higher.

When I sent Mark on a sheep herding task I let go by sending him on his way without following behind him to make sure he did it correctly and later lecturing him about all he did wrong. That's how I define "let go." I knew sheep would at times be scattered and harassed. It seemed necessary to train another shepherd. Otherwise Mark would have remained as one who fed and watered the dogs while I continued to attempt more than I had time to do.

Having gone through that experience the summer that Mark was 13 years old, and reflecting on what really happened I realized there were three basic principles or steps to that success; Pray, Trust, and Let go. Praise the Lord: I had made no attempt to dream up some cute little formula that matched the PTL used to indicate, "Praise the Lord." Nonetheless it serves as a good guide for Christians who want to train shepherds. PTL!

15

When My Sheep Hear My Voice and Follow Me

My sheep know my voice, and I know them, and they follow me. (John 10:27)

April 1991. I called my sheep and got just the response I expected. There were only about thirty or forty sheep on top of the hill that I could see, but I knew if they came to me, the other two hundred just over the hill would follow. All I needed was for a single sheep to come when I called.

They did not come. Those in view raised their heads and looked down the hill to the gate where I was standing. One sheep called back to me as she looked, but she, like the others, never moved. I could tell by her voice and by the looks on their faces that they were fully aware I was their shepherd. Yes, they responded just as I expected. They heard my voice, they knew who I was, but they did not follow me.

Sometimes my sheep do follow me when I call. They come when they are hungry. They come when they are frightened. And they come when they anticipate something better than what they now have, like a lush new pasture. They are very much creatures of habit, and they have a good memory.

During a Good Shepherd course here at Psalm 23 Camp, one of the pastures had begun to get a bit depleted because the sheep had been grazing there for several days. I told the group of pastors how the sheep would probably act when I called. Predictably, they looked up at the sound of my voice, and some even called back. But none came to the gate where I wished to let them in to graze on the lush new grass. After several unsuccessful attempts to get them to come, I sent my sheep dogs to bring the sheep to me so we could move them into the new pasture. They were afraid of the dogs and came running to me.

The next day, the sheep were back grazing in the old pasture, and I informed the group that we would likely get a totally different response this time. Sure enough, when I called out to the flock there was an immediate lifting of heads, many calls back, and nearly a stampede as they ran toward the gate to the new pasture. They knew what to expect.

Jesus said, "My sheep know my voice, and I know them, and they follow me." (John 10:27). He did not simply say, "My sheep follow me." Nor did He stop at, "My sheep know my voice." In other words, Jesus indicated that those who hear also follow.

Why do my sheep fail to follow me at times? Unlike the shepherds of old, we do not lead our sheep out to pasture daily. Shepherds in biblical days sometimes put their sheep in the folds at night with sheep belonging to other shepherds. Each morning the shepherd led his own sheep out to graze, and they followed his voice wherever he led them. I, however, am not a constant companion. Our relationship is not consistent, and they do not depend upon me to lead them to a pasture every day.

When spring comes and we have the lush green pastures, my sheep hardly acknowledge that I am in the field when

I call them. I might as well be whistling Dixie. But let my sheep get hungry and they will stampede toward my call. If I allow them to have a treat one day, like greener grass or some tasty grain, they will come running when I call the next day.

If I were to call my sheep three days in succession to put them through a routine checkup, a parasite treatment, or some other procedure that would be for their welfare, they would stop following because they were not being fed.

We Christians are like that so much of the time. We like the treats, and we come running when we are hungry or frightened. Yet we hear testimony after testimony of Christians who moved away from God's lush pastures, following their noses instead of their Shepherd. Some testify that they knew God was calling them for a long, long time to do a certain thing, yet they resisted.

You see, we don't like the working chute with its accompanying vaccinations, the inspections for ailments, or the medicine for microscopic parasites that so often inhabit the pasture. We would much rather just let Jesus swing the gate wide open each day to a fresh, green, lush, tender new growth of pasture where we can get our fill quickly and then move over under the canopy of a huge shade tree to keep us comfortable through the hot part of the day.

Like the sheep, our well being is a whole lot better if we follow Jesus daily, and not just at the times when we know good things are going our way. And when times are good, we need to make Him the first choice each day, rather than wait until disaster strikes and count on Him as a last resort.

The message of the gospel is bringing new souls into the Kingdom by the thousands in Russia, Central America, the Philippines, and in other countries where there is a deep, deep spiritual hunger. And at the same time, the gospel is falling on many deaf ears in the United States. Have the people in America been like the sheep in a springtime pasture, ignoring the call of the Shepherd? Do we not realize there are often sacrifices to be made, days when we must leave the green pasture and pass through His working chute? Do we not realize the lush green grass on which we are so contentedly feeding may have become contaminated with those invisible yet destructive parasites?

Do we hear His voice, but merely raise our heads while chewing a mouthful of grass? Do we look His way for a moment or two, ignoring the call as we return to graze at the spot where we stand? Or are we like the sheep described in John 10:27, when Jesus said, "My sheep hear my voice, and they follow me."?

16

What Do You Do with a Fat Sheep?

Therefore this is what the Sovereign LORD says to them: See, I myself will judge between the fat sheep and the lean sheep. (Ezekiel 34:20).

Summer 1991. Animal science students learn that nutrients consumed by sheep are used in a number of ways depending on their age, physical condition, production level, diet, and other factors. Animals always use some nutrients for maintenance such as activity of the heart and lungs. Any nutrients above what the animal needs for maintenance can be used for things like wool, meat, and milk production. Pregnant females have special nutrient needs, and working animals, such as our Border Collie sheep-herding dogs, use a tremendous amount of energy for the work they perform.

God gave animals the capacity to store excess energy for emergency purposes in the form of body fat. In simple terms, if all the requirements of a sheep have been met for maintenance, pregnancy, milk, meat, wool, and work (sheep are sometimes used as draft animals), any excess nutrients can be stored as fat.

Lactation is the most demanding of normal physiological functions in ewes. A ewe in full production will normally loose weight because the demand for nutrients to produce milk for the lamb exceeds what she can physically ingest. As a shepherd observes his flock in late summer his eyes will detect some ewes that are overly fat. This is often an indication that the ewe has grazed all summer with no lamb nursing her. The sheep becomes fat because she is consuming much but producing little to nothing. What do I do with a fat sheep? I sell her!

Many jokes are made about our lack of discipline as human beings, our overeating, dieting, and the never-ending struggle to maintain a desired body weight. We Americans just eat too much for the demands of our bodies.

Spiritually speaking, what do you do with a fat sheep? The United States of America has the most abundant Christian resources in the entire world with its surplus of Bibles, church buildings, trained ministers, seminaries, Christian radio and television broadcasts, books, magazines, audio and video tapes in addition to Christian conferences, seminars, rallies, revivals, courses, concerts, camps, and all kinds of programs. Plus, we have the bookmarks, bumper stickers, flags, greeting cards, plaques, and Bible School supplies, etc. found at Christian books stores. Would I be amiss in saying that we have the opportunity to become spiritually fat?

A survey compiled by Christian musician Keith Green, revealed some startling facts about Christians. In the United States we have one Christian worker for every 230 people while the rest of the world has one Christian worker for every 450,000 people! Are we fat with Christian workers?

A 1991 survey by David Barrett revealed more interesting statistics. For example, some 90 percent of all the evangelistic efforts in the world is directed toward Christians, not the lost. That is remarkable considering the fact that about one quarter of the world's population is ignorant of Christianity. And, with all our Christian resources, what have we produced? It's no secret that the U.S. is in a state of moral decline. It's no secret that we, as a people, have turned our back on God to look to the government for provision, security, and comfort. We have become a nation of fat, lazy sheep.

Experience has taught me how to identify the signs of a non-producing sheep. The sheep that is fat because she did not birth a lamb and give it milk for growth has no place in our pastures. These sheep are sold, and from the sale barn most will go directly to a slaughterhouse.

The Bible says, "You have lived on earth in luxury and self-indulgence. You have fattened yourselves in the day of slaughter." (James 5:5) The Bible also says, "—You are always on their lips but far from their hearts. – Drag them off like sheep to be butchered! Set them apart for the day of slaughter!" (Jeremiah 12:2-3)

Perhaps a more appropriate verse is James 4:17, "Anyone, then who knows the good he ought to do and doesn't do it, sins." We have plenty of opportunities to be productive, and the choice is up to us. Are we going to feed His sheep, or merely feed ourselves?

17

Until the Soil Warms

Let us not become weary in doing good, for at the proper time we will reap a harvest if we do not give up.
(Galatians 6:9)

September 1991. In much the same manner that a young child makes frequent trips to his newly planted garden, I often visited a steep hillside sheep pasture here at Psalm 23 Camp looking for emerging sprouts. Differences are that I am many years past being a child, and I have planted seeds on many occasions. Nonetheless, I was acting a bit like a child; I checked the soil frequently and became a bit disappointed when I failed to find seedlings rising from the soil.

I had broadcast grass seed in February by a method called frost seeding. The seeds work their way into the soil with alternating periods of freezing and thawing. This particular year began to be a disappointment to me as I failed to find plant growth when I had predicted (based on previous experiences) the seedlings would be seen.

Then to my surprise, some time in late spring I found abundant growth on that hillside. I had passed through a period of expectancy, followed by a period of doubt, then a period of serous doubt that the seeds would ever emerge as living plants. Then there was a period of realization that the seed sowing had been a success even though I had such doubts.

So what happened? Why did I fail to see results as in past years? What had caused this predictable phenomenon to suddenly shake my faith? As I attempted to analyze what happened, I suddenly realized that we had an unusually cool spring. You see the seeds do not germinate and emerge from the soil until the moist soil warms up enough to awaken the seed from its dormancy. That was the reason the predictable became unpredictable – the plant seed will not germinate until the soil warms.

What about your faith, Christian? Are you like me, preferring to have a light switch faith, or are you willing to wait until the soil warms? Occasionally I hear someone describe faith using the example of electricity that gives light when we move a switch. Even though we do not understand electricity, we have faith the light will come on when we flip the switch. However it doesn't take a lot of faith when the light comes on immediately 999 times out of 1000 flips.

Have you ever exercised your faith about some situation such as God's healing your body or that of another and then seen the prayer of faith answered? Have you then had a similar situation arise later, except you have yet to see results? Do you ever grow weary because you are unable to see results when you want to see them?

I know of a small group of people, who as missionaries to a foreign country saw rapid growth with respect to souls being birthed into the Kingdom of God. Later they traveled to a neighboring country only to spend an entire year without a soul won to the Lord. However within ten years there were hundreds, perhaps thousands, who came to know Jesus even though none were won the first year. The conditions between the two countries were different. Perhaps the soil had to warm.

In his letter to the Galatians, Paul said, "Let us not become weary in doing good, for at the proper time we will reap a harvest if we do not give up." (Gal. 6:9) Are you sowing spiritual seed into your life, or the lives of your children, grand children, friends and others? Do you do this and then become a bit weary when you fail to see growth? The Bible says only God can make things grow. (1 Cor. 3:7) In essence you and I will likely have those times when we just have to wait for God's proper time – perhaps we will have to wait until the soil warms.

18

Shepherd at the Gate

Enter through the narrow gate. For wide is the gate and broad is the road that leads to destruction, and many enter through it. But small is the gate and narrow the road that leads to life and only a few find it. (Matthew 7:13-14)

Fall 1991. There was a slope down the hill and then a fence in a flat area approximately three hundred feet away. Beyond the fence lay a swamp, a small stream, another fence, a narrow field, a third fence, a gentle slope upward, and finally a large flock of sheep on the hillside. This was the view that a lone sheep had as she stood on a different hill.

    We often move sheep from one pasture to another. Seldom is this done without the assistance of one or more of our sheep dogs. It is not unusual to gather the flock, only to have one or more sheep that fail to exit the field with the rest of the flock. Such was the occasion I now describe. I stood at the gate as I usually do while the flock came to me. They passed through the gate, walked a short distance, crossed a bridge over the stream, and the dogs and I directed them through a second gate to a hillside pasture.

It wasn't long before I heard the voice of a sheep left alone, a bleating voice I all too often recognize. It was the voice of a lost sheep, a sheep suddenly left all alone. There was no immediate danger. No life-threatening predator was in pursuit. It was just a voice of loneliness as a sheep suddenly realizes other sheep are not nearby. Even though some such sheep have an independent spirit that causes them to wander too far from the flock, the response is still the same when they stop eating or exploring long enough to realize they are all alone. At that point they begin to search for the comfort of the flock

I stood by the gate and listened. Suddenly, I saw her coming over the hilltop. She was facing my direction and was about three hundred feet away from me. I immediately called to her. The sheep looked at me, and I'm sure she heard my voice. But she also had, by that time, seen the flock of sheep on the distant hill. The temptation was too great. The ewe attempted to join the flock by walking directly toward them through the impassible obstacles rather than coming to me to pass through the gate. Many implications can be drawn from the behavior of this sheep. The Bible says, "Enter through the narrow gate. For wide is the gate and broad is the road that leads to destruction, and many enter through it. But small is the gate and narrow the road that leads to life, and only a few find it." (Matthew 7:13-14)

The flock of sheep that day was safe in the pasture because they got there by following my lead. They took the long way around the obstacles by coming through the narrow gate where I stood. The road that took them across a bridge was also narrow. That gave them a way of passing the swamp and then crossing the stream.

David drew on his experiences tending sheep as a boy when he described the Lord as his Shepherd. The words "he restores my soul – he guides me in paths of righteousness" are certainly descriptive of the role so often played by the shepherd (see Psalm 23:3). It seems that sheep easily go astray, get left behind, become entangled in fences, or get into some other kind of trouble when they go their own way. Sheep are often in need of restoration.

As a shepherd, I find that sheep need each other, but restoration seldom prevails in the absence of a shepherd. A sheep that is separated might be able to return to the flock after going through fences and traversing swamps, but there is an easier way – by going to the shepherd at the gate.

We know that people are much like sheep. We need the fellowship of others. However, following others is useless in terms of eternal life unless we have a personal response to the Shepherd. Much of the false teaching today centers around the idea of unity, the unity of all religions. I have heard people say that we should pray to God "as we know Him," as if there is more than one way to the one true God.

Everyone at times feels a sense of loneliness. Like lonely sheep in a pasture we begin to search. In full view on the hillside are the people we often look to for leadership. We want to be a part of that crowd. We want the comfort and security of acceptance by our peers. And believe me, peer pressure is not just a teenage problem. I've seen plenty of adults get into trouble by trying to fit in with the crowd.

The sheep that attempted to join the flock that day reminded me of the condition of many people in the United Slates with regard to religion and lifestyle, which in reality are one and the same. In other words, your lifestyle is your religion. The Bible says, "For where your treasure is, there your heart will be also." (Matthew 6:21) We have a follow-the-flock mentality – try to keep up with the Jones's, which has led to a long list of destructive consequences, a broad road, as it were.

This was made clearer to me as I visited one day with sixteen-year-old Ben Trolese. Ben grew up in Nicaragua, where his parents work as missionaries. Although they visited the United States on occasion, Ben told me he was convinced that life is better for him and other people in the poverty-stricken country of Nicaragua. Why? He said there were too many distractions in the Untied States, our emphasis on material things and our time spent seeking personal pleasure. He thought it would be more difficult for young people in the Untied States to have a strong committed personal relationship with Jesus Christ.

The more we focus on material possessions, the more things we buy. We buy and buy until by and by our heart is with our treasure. The more pleasure people seek, the more corrupt the forms of pleasure become. Our lifestyles tend to conform to those of the crowd. If a fast-food chain sells a stuffed monkey to go with the hamburger, many kids will soon have a stuffed monkey, and eventually it seems all the other kids will also want one. The pattern continues over and over until it leads to destruction when youth evolve into adults who put their treasure in things.

Ben Trolese was right. Many of us have gotten caught up in one worldly thing after another. We find ourselves tangled in the fences and bogged down in the swamps as we attempt to get to the rest of the flock. Many people are longing for the peace and contentment they see in Christians, but they travel the wrong paths in search of that happiness. The only way is through the gate. And Jesus said in John 10:9, "I am the gate; whoever enters through me will be saved. He will come in and go out, and find pasture." Jesus also said that the sheep that follow him will have eternal life and never perish. (John 10:27) "No one comes to the Father except through me." (John 14:6) The fences and the swamp can represent eternal separation from God for those who refuse to follow the voice of the Shepherd. The lost, unsaved don't have a chance on the broad path.

Christians can also encounter fences and swamps when we refuse to completely surrender our lives to the Lordship of Jesus Christ. We need that daily in and out of His pasture. Yesterday's pasture will not carry us through today. We cannot be effective disciples when we are bogged down in the swamp or caught up in the fence. There are no short cuts; we must discipline ourselves to keep a keen eye on the Shepherd at the gate rather than the flock on the hillside.

19

Conditions are Right for What Grows There

But among you there must not be even a hint of sexual immorality, or of any kind of immorality, or of any kind of impurity, or of greed, because these are improper for God's holy people. (Ephesians 5:3)

Summer 1992. A lot of thistles were in pasture fields in this area during the 1992 growing season. This followed the worst drought in many years, the 1991 growing season. The sod in some areas could have been swept away with a leaf rake because the dry weather had caused roots to die. I don't know for certain, but these conditions with the dead sod probably helped create an ideal seedbed for thistles to grow in the season to follow.

Grassland farmers are continually challenged, because they have so few controls over the many variables that affect plant growth. Unlike the grain farmer who drives machinery over the field to prepare the soil, apply seed, fertilizer and herbicides to control conditions, the grassland farmer is often trying to manage pastures with many circumstances beyond his control, such as rocks, trees, ravines, streams and steep grades.

Thistles, as well as many other plants, are undesirable in a pasture. Yet there are also many good plant species found in pastures. As a starting point to obtain the desirable species, we must determine why we have the ones that are in a field, be they good or bad. The first thing we must understand is that no matter what is growing in a pasture at any point in time, desirable or undesirable, the conditions are right for what is growing there.

Christians should grasp that principle. Far too often Christians attempt to go forward with a limited knowledge of the conditions that have brought us to the place where we are now. For example, right now America stands in a tremendous patch of thistles. I understand why our educational institutions, our governmental agencies and the secular media react the way they do. They attempt to analyze our situation with worldly eyes. They may see the thistles and attempt to be rid of them. However, cutting a thistle down is striking out at a manifestation, whereas we need to change the conditions that lead to the growth in the beginning. The truth is that cutting the thistle may do little in the long run. We must know more about the conditions that started the growth.

In our society there has been much talk for several years about deliberate abortion of unborn babies. Even Christians fail to agree if a woman should have a right to have such an abortion. In truth, the problem centers on sexual activity outside the bounds of marriage vows. Pregnancy out of wedlock is simply a manifestation. There are many, many variables in our culture that prepared "the seedbed" for this particular circumstance. However, for practical purposes, most people who want women to have a choice to abort a child in reality are actually condoning sexual intercourse between unmarried people. In other words, freedom from restraints of sexual activity is a condition that has lead to an issue of what I shall call life versus "anti-life" of children before they are born.

The same condition, sexual freedom, has grown such idiotic "trash in the pasture" as teaching teens to practice safe sex, and schooling elementary students on the merits of homosexuality, as if these are normal alternatives. When I began teaching college students over 20 years ago I saw some disturbing seeds being planted in our young people. Now the people in our schools are being taught by the generation I saw 20 years ago. I'm suggesting that most of the problems we have come from the seeds of earlier generations. God's sowing and reaping principle works. I see a very direct relationship, cause/effect, sowing/reaping, between the two generations.

I heard a political candidate say family values were not an important issue during this presidential election year, and that the economy is our most important issue. I can understand why a man might say that and believe it. The Bible says, "The man without the Spirit does not accept the things that come from the Spirit of God, for they are foolishness to him, and he cannot understand them, because they are spiritually discerned." (1 Cor. 2:14) The poor economy is merely the manifestation of an ungodly people; it's a thistle that has helped bring the pasture to ruin. We need to ask the question, "What conditions lead to the growth of this problem?"

Why is it safe to say a poor economy has grown because of ungodliness? There is simply no way a people can lie, steal and cheat, and expect the economy to prosper. It matters not whether we look at something as large as the scandals that have occurred in the savings and loan companies, or something small as the employee who pads his expense account or takes a sick day to go shopping. It should be obvious to us that it will take more than an election to change things – we need to focus on the conditions that prepared the seedbed for the crop we are now harvesting. Furthermore, that is a distinct responsibility of the church (all Christians), not the government.

To a large extent, we Christians have been as much of the problem as others have in providing improper conditions for growth. It's a little like spending a lot of time in a smoke filled room and walking out not realizing you now smell like smoke. But as you get around those who have not been in the smoke, they smell the odor on your clothing, while you no longer smell it because it has become a part of you.

The Bible says, "But among you there must not be even a hint of sexual immorality, or of any kind of immorality, or of any kind of impurity, or of greed, because these are improper for God's holy people." (Eph 5:3) Sexual immorality gets a lot of attention from pulpits and publications, such as this one, but take note that God's Word puts greed right along beside sexual immorality as being improper for God's holy people. What makes that bit of Scripture more striking is the phrase "even a hint." Does that mean that even a hint of greed is improper for God's holy people?

Let's be honest. Yes, Americans, including Christians, in the past few decades have had a hint of immorality, impurity and greed. Could those be primary conditions for growth that caused us to be, at this point, standing among the thistles?

A farmer can't change the crop that's already matured. Neither can Christians. However, we can do something about the next crop. Let us be wise enough to understand where to begin – the Bible: "This is what we speak, not in words taught us by human wisdom but in words taught by the Spirit –." (1 Cor 2:13)

20

Night Watch

It will be good for those servants whose master finds them ready even if he comes in the second or third watch of the night. (Luke 12:38)

Winter 1992. Did you ever wonder why Jesus was born at night? Do you suppose it has any significance to the fact that even now Jesus comes to people during a period of darkness? Did you ever give thought to why shepherds were the first to receive news of the birth of the Savior? Do you think it was all coincidence, or did God's plan provide for such? Was the glory of the Lord for all to see, but only discernible by those who were awake and keeping watch? Look at the account in Luke 2:8.

And there were shepherds living out in the fields nearby, keeping watch over their flocks at night.

Before looking closely at the Scripture I wish to make a few points about the responsibility a shepherd has to watch over the flock. Providing protection from predators, elements of weather, insects and diseases, hazards of becoming snared by brush, fence wire, streams, and being cast on their backs (a sheep cannot always get up if it rolls on to its back with feet sticking straight up) are a few of the things I must watch for in my flock.

A good shepherd will have an acute sense of discernment; he will be ever watchful to detect abnormalities in the flock. I don't claim to be a good shepherd, but I know enough about sheep to recognize some good traits in a shepherd. The eyes, the ears, and ability to recognize even the most subtle changes in the flock are the shepherd's means of keeping watch.

Earlier this day in December I traveled by tractor across the farm to feed a portion of our flock that is in the valley. As I traveled that half mile or so I very carefully looked to the high mountain pastures to see if I could locate two other smaller bands (or flocks) of sheep that are still out grazing and are not fed hay daily. Each band has many acres in which to graze, and cannot be seen at all times from the valley. I did not rest until I had sighted each band. Even though they were a half-mile away high in the hills, I concluded they were okay. Knowing the weather conditions the night before, the direction of the cold winds, and a number of other variables, I knew within reasonable limits, what to expect in terms of the location of the sheep, their behavior, etc. Frequent checks on the flock with an ever-watchful eye are necessary to know the condition of the flock and detect potential problems.

Night watch is no fun. It requires a lot of sacrifice of my personal comfort. It requires that I be out in the field with the sheep. I must be awake and alert, and my sense of hearing must be sensitized. It is very difficult, particularly if I am alone, because sleep eventually overtakes me. I seldom keep watch at night and only after predators have been in the flock. When I do, I usually spend the night in a pickup truck with a loaded rifle. Predators and sheep make little noise during an attack. The thundering hoof beats of running sheep, or perhaps the squeaking sound of sheep running into wire fences are among the few sounds one can detect during an attack at night.

Now let's look closely at the Scripture mentioned above. There are four features about Luke 2:8 that I wish to call to your attention. (1) There was more than one shepherd. (2) They were living in the fields. (3) They were keeping watch. (4) It was night.

First, focus on number two. It is tough living in the fields. The wind chill here last night, was somewhere around zero degrees F. It is much more comfortable in this house where there is plenty of heat. It is more comfortable here at a computer, soft seats nearby, the coffee pot close at hand, etc. In case you haven't caught up with where this is going, here it is – the shepherd in a comfortable house is an accurate description of Christians in the United States. All professing Christians don't fit the same mold, but any who wish to study the facts, examine the statistics, or cast a watchful eye across different flocks, sub-flocks and bands of sheep in the valleys and on the mountains of this land, and among all nations of the world with a discerning mind under guidance of the Holy Spirit, will likely agree that we are a nation of indoor shepherds while the lost sheep are out in the fields.

Sheep are easier to see when you live out in the fields with the flock. I have a view from my desk that puts into focus a portion of the land where my sheep graze. It offers some, but not enough view for me to keep careful watch over my sheep. I might add that it would offer even less (none to be exact) if this window were made of stained glass. A few days ago my neighbor Larry Echols called to tell me he had seen a coyote near my sheep. One of the best neighbors a shepherd can have is another shepherd. Larry understands the importance of keeping watch over a flock because he too is a shepherd. We communicate with one another any time we see potential danger to our flocks. Church congregations need discernment on how to work together particularly during these days where darkness looms so heavy in this world. When we choose to be independent of others we are apt to fall asleep at some point during the night.

All watching, particularly as the Bible tells us, is not for guarding. Although the shepherds near Bethlehem on that infamous night were keeping watch over their flocks they also saw the glory of the Lord shone around them (Luke 2:9), they heard the good news of great joy (vs. 10), about the birth of a Savior, Christ the Lord (vs. 11) and they were told of a sign (vs. 12) for identification of this baby. Furthermore, the shepherds visited the baby lying in a manger (vs. 16), and at that point they spread the word (vs. 17) and then returned, glorifying and praising God (vs. 20). I repeat an earlier question; was the glory of the Lord for all to see, but only discernible to those who were awake and keeping watch?

Are we willing to take the night watch working with other shepherds? During New Testament times there were supposedly four three-hour night watches between 6:00 p.m. and 6:00 a.m. I'm afraid we are guilty of wanting to stay with the day watch. As a matter of fact we are inclined to want to narrow that down to one or two hours in a day, and Sunday is the only day we want to participate. If the glory of God came at the third night watch would we see it, or would we sleep through it?

Do take note that keeping watch by night necessitates living in the fields. Are we willing to go beyond the comfortable pews and stained glass windows into the fields where the harvest is ripe? Living in the fields with the sheep is not easy. Try ministering to the homeless in New York City or the Muslims in Iraq.

Do we claim God has called us to a computer with a limited view of sheep out the window, a place not too cold or too hot, one that is close to soft cushions, a coffee pot, and a sweet roll or two? Why not throw in a good salary with fringes. Or we could throw in enough money to buy the stained glass to completely block the view of the fields and the sheep therein. At that point we could just forget about the sheep out there altogether and concentrate more on our own comfort.

Has God called a disproportionate number of Christians to minister in the United States with millions of un-shepherded sheep in the rest of the world? He did command us to make disciples of **all** nations. Maybe we would have received a different sign or call on our lives had we not fallen asleep during the night watch. Constant care, feeding and protection of sheep can only be fulfilled when a night watch is a part of the flock management. In a like manner we are to be prepared for His Second Coming. Are you and I willing to commit to a night watch? God's Word always says it best – Jesus said, "It will be good for those servants whose master finds them ready even if he comes in the second or third watch of the night." (Luke 12:38)

21

Front Feet Bound, Lying on Her Side

– he restores my soul. He guides me in paths of righteousness for his name's sake. (Psalm 23:3)

Winter 1992. Young, strong, healthy, good condition, but she lay helpless on her side because her front feet were bound. I was at least one-fourth mile away when I spotted what appeared to be a dead sheep. As I drew close to her I realized this lifeless appearing ewe was actually alive. I concluded her lifeless appearance was the result of a long period of struggle trying to get free. The struggle to get free had left her exhausted.

My arrival saved her life. My chore to free her was simple. Other sheep could not free her; my sheep dogs could not free her; but a fairly simple touch released her from the fence into a path of righteousness to return to the flock less than 300 feet away. To me the whole incident well represents the condition of the U.S.A., a nation on the brink of exhaustion.

America was young, strong, healthy, and in good condition until – she did what my sheep did – she challenged the boundary line placed for her protection. My ewe had challenged a sturdy and well-defined fence. In this case greed was likely what motivated her to go beyond the boundary I had constructed.

America; young, strong and healthy, but now lying on her side, front feet bound, helpless and going nowhere as long as she is bound. She is in that condition because she chose to step outside the boundary given in God's Word.

The knowledge of 10,000 Ph.D.s, the passage of 10,000 bills in congress, the establishment of 10,000 new school board policies, the power of 10,000 nuclear reactors, the incorporation of 10,000 improvements in computer technology would be as a sheep with its front feet bound, flopping around helplessly unless we yield to and accept the Lord Jesus as our Shepherd for He "restores my soul. He guides me in paths of righteousness for his name's sake."(Ps. 23-3)

22

Each Dog Doing His Own Thing

Am I now trying to win the approval of men, or of God? Or am I trying to please men? If I were still trying to please men, I would not be a servant of Christ. (Galatians 1:10)

Spring 1992. It was chaotic; it seldom occurs, but it was one of those times when the sheep became scattered after I entered the field with our three sheep-herding dogs, Queenie, Dottie, and King. Normally the sheep flow together, the dogs work together and we proceed with the plans I have for the sheep. But for some unexplained reason the sheep began to scatter and my attempts to have them brought together as one unit by giving commands to the dogs failed. In fact, it just made matters worse.

At that point I settled down a bit, looked around at the situation and I began to see some interesting parallels in the church. One shepherd, three sheep dogs, and more than three hundred sheep in the pasture that day seemed to represent much of what we see in the body of Christ today.

I saw about 40 to 50 sheep in one corner of the field with Queenie intently keeping watch that they did not leave that corner. A few hundred feet away Dottie had sheep held in another corner with her eyes fixed on them. Each of those two dogs had their back to me. King was near the center of the field appearing to be about as confused as the sheep, the remainder of which were scattered over the field. The primary analogy I saw between that situation and Christians is that each dog was doing their own thing, no matter what my commands were.

I noticed that Queenie and Dottie were doing an excellent job at keeping their respective groups held in corners of the field. Queenie was nearest to me and I noticed that she had a determination that was so intense that should some poor sheep try to escape that corner the dog would surely tear a leg off such a dumb animal. What made matters worse was that she also had her back to me which eliminated the possibility of seeing any hand signals I might want to give.

On occasion I have one or more dogs hold sheep in a corner of a field. Usually it's a time when I wish to be among the sheep to catch one of them for close observation. A dog's ability to hold the sheep in the corner is of immense value at times such as that. However a dog that does an excellent job at a task is of no value to me as a shepherd unless that is what I want done at that time. If I wish to move 300 sheep out of a field then one dog's demonstration of his superb ability to hold sheep in a corner may impress someone, but not me at that moment.

How many of us are on this earth doing a good job at the task before us, but in reality are like sheep dogs guarding our group just daring one to move the wrong direction? How often do we exhibit the zeal of a Border Collie sheep dog, and how often do we in our pride-filled hearts think what a great job we are doing for God? How often do we do these things with such diligence and over such a long period of time that we fail to realize that we have positioned ourselves where we never lose sight of the sheep in front of us but we now have the Good Shepherd to our back? Individuals do it, congregations do it, denominations do it, and educational institutions do it. All of us at times do an excellent job in man's eyes, but the question is, "Who, or what spirit is directing the activity?" Is it the Holy Spirit? Is it a deceiving spirit? Why have so many colleges and universities that were started by the church abandoned Christianity? We can make all manner of excuses about money, changes in society, etc. but the question still remains, "Was God giving the commands when changes were being made?"

We can do things to please ourselves, to please others, and to please God. The Bible has many scriptures that say we are to please God. The apostle Paul asked some pertinent questions, "Am I now trying to win the approval of men, or of God? Or am I trying to please men? If I were still trying to please men, I would not be a servant of Christ." (Gal. 1:10) Our problems often arise when we fail to distinguish between pleasing God and pleasing man. We think we are pleasing God and pleasing man. We think we are doing something to please God when in fact we have done little more than occupy a corner of the pasture. The Bible says, "Do nothing out of selfish ambition or vain conceit –." (Php. 2:3) No doubt some men take their God given abilities and add to that some training. Then perhaps a vision comes to win the lost. But some men get caught up in the frenzy as my dogs did and loose sight and sound of the Shepherd. God's vision has changed to man's vision; selfish ambition! Does Isaiah 56:11 fit here? "They are dogs with mighty appetites; they never have enough; they are shepherds who lack understanding; they all turn to their own way, each seeks his own gain."

Many of us select a church to attend out of selfish ambition – we want to hear a preacher who says from the pulpit what our itching hears want to hear. Sure, we want to hear something from the Bible, but we prefer it only be from selected verses of the Bible. We wish to be edified. We want to leave the church building feeling good. Most of us don't care for the hard sayings. I find it interesting that Paul, in his second letter to Timothy said that "All Scripture is God-breathed and is useful for teaching, rebuking, correcting, and training for righteousness–." (3:16). Rebuking and correcting we don't like, but note that represents two of four things mentioned. Furthermore Paul wrote, "Preach the Word; correct, rebuke and encourage." (4:2). Correct and rebuke is two out of three.

Our selfish desires have lead to the proliferation of a lot of corners in the pasture, if you will. Shepherds of the day have obliged us by giving us what we want, which explains why we hear of terms such as social gospel, soft gospel, cosmetic gospel, partial gospel, and prosperity gospel. I was in a Sunday school class once where one prominent man in the church told the class he didn't want to come to Sunday school if the teacher used the Bible to teach. On the other extreme we find some people spend a lot to time going to church meetings, listening to cassette tapes, reading Christian books, reading and studying the Bible, but who seemingly never learn enough to start acting on it.

I am familiar with a few Christian schools near here and I have made it a point to ask leaders if they get much support from other churches to develop and maintain their school. I learned that others are reluctant to assist, particularly if represented by a different denomination. Are Christian schools important? Sure they are! Then why do churches not work together with the prayer and financial support needed in these schools? If these are questions on your mind may I suggest you check the pasture? I think churches often neglect Christian schools for the same reason they fail to work together on other things – they are in respective corners and each dog is doing his own thing.

King set an example that captured my heart. Remember I said he was in the middle of the field and seemed to be as confused as the sheep? There is good reason for that; he was trying desperately to keep an eye on me midst all the scattered sheep, the various commands and general confusion. Despite all the chaos he was still seeking my specific instructions. You see, King was doing his own thing too — he doesn't like to proceed without clear-cut, specific instructions from his master. He didn't create the confusion; he just got caught in it. But he didn't arbitrarily begin cornering sheep either.

My under-shepherds are gifted and they are trained. But two other characteristics are also very important. First they must be aware of my presence and my commands, and second, and most important, they must be obedient to those commands. My intent that day in the pasture was to have all the sheep move in the same direction with the under-shepherds doing the work based upon my commands. Do you suppose this is parallel to what our Lord wants for us?

God has gifted you and me. You and I are to act according to His will and direction and not display our talents in a corner just because we know we can. You may have the God given ability to direct a crew to build a tower of Babel, but does that mean that is what you are to do? Of course not!

As we move toward the close of the twentieth century it is obvious that turmoil and confusion abound within as well as outside the body of Christ. Christians, especially those in positions of leadership, need to stand on the Word of God and always position themselves so they can see and hear the Master. King's willingness to stand in the middle of so much confusion that day in the pasture and still focus on my direction will no doubt serve as a model for me to remember for a long time.

23

Hey Shepherd, Do You Smell Like a Sheep?

−This is what the Sovereign Lord says: 'Woe to the shepherds of Israel who only take care of themselves! Should not shepherds take care of the flock?'
(Ezekiel 34:2)

Fall 1992. I probably smell more like a sheep now than I did two or three years ago. The reason is simple; I am spending more time with the sheep. The reason I spend more time is also simple. Economically, the sheep industry has been at rock bottom for about two years. Attempts to do something about the economic squeeze must include better management, which necessarily means spending more time with the sheep. To add insult to injury, coyotes have invaded this geographic area and given shepherds a challenge for which we were not prepared. We routinely put some, if not all, of our sheep up in a sheep fold, as it were, every night to protect them from coyotes. One benefit of this daily gathering of sheep is that I get to know them better, which can be good in the long run, for them and for me.

I heard a story about a pastor who was given a Cadillac automobile. It supposedly caused all manner of havoc in his church. The implication was that people in the congregation were jealous because of the blessing the pastor received. That is about all of the details I heard, but I immediately chuckled inside as I heard the account being told. I chuckled, not because of the situation of a disturbed congregation, nor because he received the fancy automobile. I just thought it was a bit humorous that neither the pastor who received the car nor the person telling the story had enough discernment about them to realize the effect of such a gift to the pastor. Since I don't know the situation, I don't know whether the people in the congregation were jealous or not. They may have reacted as I probably would; upset at the poor judgment of the pastor.

In recent years I have had a special interest in prosperity among Christian leaders, and how they handle it when it comes. I have a few interesting questions regarding the man who received the Cadillac. Did he really have need of a car? Do the people in his congregation drive Cadillacs, Lincolns and Chrysler New Yorkers, or do they drive Chevrolets, Fords and Plymouths? Did the pastor pay a tithe on this gift, or is he only to tithe at times when God blesses him with cash? Did he consider selling the car and then tithing? Did he consider refusing the gift because it might give an impression that he was being improperly elevated above the people in his congregation? (Just say "No." to expensive gifts!)

The Bible says (Duet. 14:22-27) that we are to take the tithe to the place God has chosen as a dwelling for His name. Furthermore He said if the place is too distant and you have been blessed to the extent that you cannot carry your tithe, then exchange your tithe for silver and take the silver with you and go to the place the Lord your God will choose. Of course in this case the pastor would not be able to carry one tenth of his car, but perhaps he could have driven the whole thing to church. That may not have worked too well either, because he likely would have had trouble getting the nine-tenths of his automobile back home.

There are other questions. Was there anyone else in the congregation who needed a car worse than the pastor? I could go on, but my point is that any man, be he a corporate executive, a government official, or pastor of a congregation, who gets set too much above his constituents, will eventually loose the "smell of sheep" on his clothing. This type life style will eventually prove harmful to the flock.

A few years ago I read the account a well-known minister wrote about a Rolex watch that was given to him. The watch was supposedly worth about $15,000. At some point later he "blessed" some other preacher by giving it to him. Ultimately the first preacher received a new watch of similar value as a gift from someone else. His point was that God not only blessed him with an expensive watch, but God blessed him with a second watch because he gave the first one away. Wonder if either of these guys tithed their blessings? I bet the watches wouldn't keep very good time with 10 percent of the parts missing? Of course, you and I both know that people who wear such watches don't do so because they want to know what time it is. A $10 digital gives the correct time.

A whole series of questions could be raised about the prosperity preachers who drive expensive cars and trade around $15,000 watches. I'm sure there must be a lot of people who are impressed and literally "eat up" hearing those type testimonies, but it seems to me the appeal would be primarily to some who are materially rich, some who want to be materially rich, and those who search for and are apt to find gods rather than God.

If a pastor, or any Christian leader, stood before me giving Christian testimony, and I knew he had a $15,000 watch on his wrist, he would not get my ear any quicker than a man who completely disrobed himself while giving testimony. I assure you jealousy would not be involved in either case; it is a matter of poor judgment of such leaders.

Christians in positions of leadership who live in materialistic luxury above the sheep of this world have become insensitive to the needs of the flock. I suggest that these type shepherds have long ago lost the smell of sheep. They either don't know the condition of those who Jesus called "My sheep," or they don't care. "This is what the Sovereign Lord says: 'Woe to the shepherds of Israel who only take care of themselves! Should not shepherds take care of the flock?'" (Eze. 34.2) "– I myself will judge between the fat sheep and the lean sheep. Because you shove with flank and shoulder, butting all the weak sheep with your horns until you have driven them away, I will save my flock, and they will no longer be plundered." (Eze. 34:20-22)

This is a unique time in history. Our ability to communicate via satellite, with the aid of computers, phones and fax machines can literally put us in contact with the rest of the world in a manner of minutes, even seconds. There is no excuse for us to pretend we don't know what is going on throughout the world. God, in his Word, has instructed Christian leaders to "Be shepherds of God's flock that is under your care – being examples to the flock." (1Peter 5:2-3) If millions are naked and starving while shepherds are trading plunder, what example do the shepherds set? Do they really care about getting down in the sheep pen day after day, or do they prefer not to smell like a sheep?

24

How High's the Water Momma?

Whoever is thirsty, let him come; and whoever wishes, let him take the free gift of the water of life. (Revelation 22:17)

Summer 1993. Two dollars a bottle and rising. Eight ounces of water in an attractive green bottle priced at $1.95 sat on a shelf in a Washington, D.C. airport coffee shop. I was with three companions waiting for a flight to Mexico City. Our final destination was a small town in southern Mexico where I would experience my first short-term mission trip.

Inwardly I smiled because I had in a small backpack a quart bottle of water that was probably from the same underground source back in West Virginia. I had heard all the stories about impure water in Third World countries. Although I knew that my quart of water from home would not last long, it provided some comfort knowing I had that little quantity. I was familiar with the brand name of the bottled water at the airport. That company is one of four within 10 miles of our farm that have tapped into the pure water that flows so abundantly from numerous springs on Peter's Mountain, the longest mountain ridge in West Virginia.

Ten such springs are found along the Living Waters Trail here at Psalm 23 Camp. One spring here at Psalm 23 runs continuously to three livestock watering tanks and still has an excess daily overflow of about 25,000 gallons. A much, much larger spring from my uncle's property supplies the water to his house, our house, the house of my parents, Psalm 23 Camp, more livestock tanks, plus one of the commercial water companies.

That bit of background concerning the abundant supply of pure spring water we have here perhaps explains to you why I had that inward smile at the airport. With thousands of gallons flowing daily from the mountain above our home, water at $2.00 a bottle seems comical. A personal joking comment I make at times when I see a familiar five-gallon water dispenser in local businesses goes something like this; "The water you have in that container is the same water we flush down our commodes at home." It is the truth as I then explain that the water in their dispenser comes from the same spring that supplies our home.

One month ago our family drove across the state of Missouri to Kansas City and returned in about a week. We saw the results of some of the flooding in the area. We would never have dreamed that the same flood would still be causing such damage a month later. About three weeks ago I watched the evening news report on TV and learned that floodwaters had risen so high in Des. Moines, Iowa that the public supply of drinking water was flooded, and thus contaminated. Last night's (Aug 4) evening news showed a major party in Des Moines as the public supply of water was again safe to drink. An interesting side note is that a few days ago I saw a local TV broadcast that showed some of the Peter's Mountain water being shipped to Des Moines. How interesting that something so common as a drink of water, particularly in a land of plenty, would be cause to celebrate. Of course the motivating factor was the sudden loss of what people had grown to take for granted.

Much could and will be said about the Flood of 1993, the Blizzard of 1993, Hurricane Andrew, the California earthquake and other recent disasters. We received two separate totally unrelated letters last month from Christians in the Midwest saying, "Maybe God is trying to tell us something." In growing up I often heard my Dad say, "Them that have will lose, and them that don't have can't lose." There are many Scriptures that point to man's folly when he holds so dearly to worldly things.

One of the impressions made on farmer work team members who went with us to Bluefields, Nicaragua in February was the fact that the people seemed to have such peace and joy in the midst of extreme poverty. Those people have been through a major civil war and a major hurricane within the past 10 years. Consider this; a hurricane in the United States blows away your $150,000 house as compared to a hurricane in Nicaragua that blows away the cardboard box in which someone lives. Neither living space is but a part of the vapor that represents this life on earth, but perhaps the man who lost his cardboard box finds peace a little quicker when he hears the Gospel.

Peoples and governments are looking to the United States for Bibles, Christian literature, and other guidance in Christian principles. It seems the Gospel is in the most demand in those places where it has been so forbidden in the past. Is the Gospel like pure mountain spring water? Is it in more demand in those areas where there is no abundant supply? How ironic that foreign governments look to us for Christian school materials because we have the abundant supply, yet we forbid the same in our own public schools!

Think about it – here we are, water, water, everywhere, and not a drop to drink. We are literally up to our ears in church buildings, Christian newsletters, books, radio and TV programs, etc. much like the flood waters. The world cries for the Good News and we have trouble knowing how to give it to them in the pure form. Our rich Christian heritage has been taken for granted and now the flood of sin in our country at times seems a threat to the faithful remnant. Surely no adult Christian, particularly those past 40 years of age, will deny the backslidden condition of our country. Yet there is a peace among many Christians in the U.S. because we know what the Bible says in the final chapter of the final book, "Whoever is thirsty, let him come; and whoever wishes, let him take the free gift of the water of life." (Rev. 22:17)

25

The Lead Sheep

Christ suffered for you, leaving you an example that you should follow in his steps. (1Peter 2:21)

September 1993. After several weeks of leading a group of young sheep out to pasture each morning in a routine manner, things were suddenly disrupted. First, more explanation about the routine; then to the disruption. The young sheep, or lambs, are more vulnerable to coyote attack than the older sheep. For that reason, I weaned the lambs more than two months ago and proceeded to pasture them separately, pen them up each night, and lead them out to pasture each morning. The routine was the same each morning in that our sheep dog King always followed the sheep while I lead. We may go to a different pasture today compared to yesterday, but the method is always the same. It worked very well until a few days ago. At that time I placed some older sheep in with the lambs, but the entire group was still 90 percent lambs.

At that point the lambs followed the older sheep, and the older sheep being more familiar (or they thought so) with the farm, began going their own way. It took a lot more work by King and several days to get any reasonable routine going again.

Sheep are gregarious, which is helpful in herding or leading them, and it is best to have at least one sheep that will quickly step out and follow the shepherd. If one steps out from the group, the others will follow. Some shepherds keep a "bell wether" for that purpose. A wether is a castrated male sheep. Without the male hormones his interest in ewes is neutral. With a bell strapped to his neck, he is easy to identify. A sheep that is mature and has a close relationship with the shepherd can serve as the one who steps out from the flock to follow the shepherd. The catch is, others will follow even when a lead sheep steps out in the wrong direction. At the time I mixed the two groups of sheep I was leading the sheep for a distance of about one-half mile through four gateways to arrive at the place I wanted them to graze. Several times adult sheep would attempt to go their own way and graze before the journey was complete.

The study of sheep/shepherd relationships is much more complex than what can be covered with a written piece as short as this one, but I do wish to ask a question for all of us. Who is the lead sheep? Or, who is your lead sheep? Better yet, who is the lead sheep for your children, or grandchildren? And how about you as the lead sheep, "Who is following you?"

We are like sheep. The Bible says, "We all, like sheep have gone astray." (Isaiah 53:6). I suggest this; sometimes we go astray on our own, and other times we go astray because we follow the wrong lead sheep. The latter is perhaps more critical because many innocent, sincere sheep go the wrong way when they follow.

Consider my sheep again. The lambs in my field could have taken one of three actions. First they could have gone their own way. Second, they could have followed the older sheep. And third, they could have followed me, the shepherd.

You and I are no different. We can go our own way, we can follow some other person, or we can follow Christ. People like to identify with a visible leader. Jesus Christ is no longer here on earth as a visible shepherd. If we choose to follow a visible, in the flesh leader, then we are following another sheep. Sure, some are to be shepherds to other people, but there is only one Chief Shepherd. You may be a shepherd to some others, but you are still a sheep to Jesus. Some pastors haven't received that revelation yet.

Let's look at 1Pet 2:21 again. Three things are shown here: 1) Christ suffered for you. 2) He left you an example, and 3) you should follow in His steps. Jesus said that those who follow him will have to deny themselves (Matt 16:24). In fact He said that unless we even hate our own life we cannot be one of his disciples (Luke 14:26). When was the last time you saw a meeting for believers advertised as *Suffering of the Saints Seminar*? The fact is the victorious, abundant life, overcoming, Kingdom now topics are bigger box office attractions. Let's be real; we don't have to live a beat down, defeated life, but the Bible makes it very plain that suffering is involved when we follow in His steps.

Older sheep always take the lead. Children watch movies and TV programming that is produced by adults. Adults manufacture and sell alcohol and drugs that are used by the young. Adults teach in formal settings of schools and colleges, and we adults lead by the examples we live. Adults represent lead sheep.

Now consider church leadership. A pastor may be considered a shepherd, but he is more like a sheep than a shepherd. The lead sheep, yes, but there is more similarity between a pastor and individuals in the congregation that there is between Jesus Christ, the Chief Shepherd and the pastor. Problems often arise when we spend too much time focusing on the footsteps of another man and not enough time reading God's Word. Luke said it so well (Acts, Chapter 17) when he said the Bereans received the message eagerly and examined the Scriptures every day to see if what Paul said was true.

At one time I had a great deal of admiration for certain ministries, that I now believe to be little more than big businesses with shepherds who are polished hucksters in a gospel for gain mode. Their followers are no doubt sincere, but sincerely paying too much attention to a lead sheep and not enough attention to the Chief Shepherd. Who do you follow?

26

To Please The Master

–yet not my will, but yours be done. (Luke 22:42)

October 1993. Our family was very fortunate to acquire two well-trained working stock dogs of the Border Collie breed during the third year of our sheep production enterprise. The previous owners were moving off their farm and they knew their dogs would be happier where they could be working.

We were given a crash-training course about how to use the dogs, their characteristics, desires and needs. One of the things we were told was that the dogs just loved to work and that they delight in pleasing their master. That bit of information was certainly true. Those two dogs are now past their working days, but they were very active for about six or eight years. Our dog King is the son of Queenie, one of the two dogs we purchased.

King is now nine years old and very active. He has been a servant well beyond what I could ever deserve. When I am near him he gives his undivided attention to me. He may be 50 yards away closely watching a group of sheep with literally one eye on them and the other on me. My voice in a low volume conversational manner can be heard at unbelievable distances. Visitors are often amazed at how he has such ability and devotion.

When working the sheep in a large pasture King is frequently looking to me while he works to determine if I have a new set of directions, either a verbal or a hand signal. He works the sheep and then watches me. Continually – he works – and he watches. I know from experiences with other dogs that some get so caught up in their work that they fail to cast a look in my direction to see if I now have a different command. Not so with King; he wants that frequent assurance that he is still doing what the master wants. Wow! That is a lesson in itself for Christians!

One of the more intriguing aspects of King's desire to get the job done is his determination when there is great difficulty and danger. One command I give him is used when the sheep are tightly crowded together in a lane or working pen. At the command "Jump up," King jumps on top of the sheep and proceeds to walk across their backs toward the end of the lane or pen. The sheep are frightened by this and will move if they can. Those sheep standing in a gateway will move on through once the dog gets on their backs.

There is danger to King when he performs the "Jump up" command because once the sheep begin to move then he no longer has a place on their backs to stand or walk. Often the sheep move, King quickly falls to the ground and the frightened sheep begin to literally trample him beneath their feet as they all run through the gateway. Each time this happens I anxiously wait to see if King surfaces without harm. It is amazing to watch him perform this type task as if it were his bread and butter, or the icing on his cake, as it were. It is as if he would rather do that than eat a big chunk of red meat. At times it is difficult to believe that he would do such things knowing he could get hurt. But, that just seems to be part of his continual effort to be obedient – to please the master.

During the summer of 1993 I had a most unusual opportunity to work with a lady by the name of Linda Scarbrough. Linda and her husband Ivan began teaching school at Seneca Trail Christian Academy the same year our son Mark enrolled in that school. For four years (7th-10th grades) Mark received teaching from them. Although I knew the Scarbroughs in a parent/teacher relationship during those years, I got to know them much better during the summer of 1993 since they were both helping us plan a special camp here at Psalm 23 Camp.

During the planning stages of the camp it became evident that Linda had a serious health problem, later determined to be a brain tumor, but none of us were prepared for her untimely death on September 13, 1993 which was 50 days following her last day as a volunteer at Psalm 23 Camp.

Linda assumed several responsibilities including that of a daily teaching centered on what the Bible says about serving others. As director of the camp I was delighted at her willingness to serve the needs of the young people.

As time passed during the planning stages of the camp there were two progressions I noticed. First of all, there seemed to be outward evidence that Linda's health was steadily declining. Secondly, her determination to help seemed to be increasing. However, her conviction was not what I would call dogged or bull headed. She did not appear to be trying to prove anything to anyone. I checked with Linda frequently by phone and I often assured her that we had plenty of workers and that she need not feel obligated to hold firm to her earlier commitment to work at the camp. I was astonished at her attitude.

She had a positive attitude with a pleasant smile, and she made it clear that her life was yielded to Jesus Christ. I saw a remarkable desire in her heart to do God's will. I saw an unusual quality in Linda Scarbrough; one of total abandonment of one's circumstances in order to focus on the will of the Master. I did not know her well, but if those few weeks were representative of her total life, she undoubtedly lived to please **The Master.**

27

Steady on – Sit – Come by

The steps of a good man are ordered by the Lord
– (Psalm 37:23)

November 1993. King had his eyes fixed on me. Positioned in a straight line between the two of us was a group of about 25 sheep. The characteristics given by our Creator to this animal we call a stock dog combined with the training and experiences in King's life seem to prescribe this set of circumstances; the sheep were being stalked like hunted animals susceptible to attack by the dog if they dared venture from their position. The dog seemed willing to kill should a single sheep attempt to go in any direction other than one straight toward me.

King had been in a similar position many times where sheep were to be gathered together and brought to the shepherd. A course in high school geometry is not necessary to understand that the shortest distance between two points is a straight line. King was determined to drive the sheep straight toward me.

As stated above, King had been in a similar position many times. Notice the previous sentence says similar position not exact position. That is the key to the circumstance that day in the barn lot. People watch King work with sheep and marvel at how "smart" he is. Yes he is smart, but far from being human. Man is intelligent, but far from being God.

The following explains what made the circumstance a challenge that day. Review the situation; the sheep were between King and me, and he was driving them toward me with dogged (pardon the pun) determination. Problem – a wire fence separated the sheep from me. The sheep were in a predicament, crowded close to the fence with King attempting to drive them straight through it in order to bring the sheep to me.

King had responded that day to a voice command of "Steady on," which means he was to go directly toward the sheep to drive them. Sometimes a stock dog will act in obedience to a command, but make a slight alteration using his own instinct or judgment. That day, for example, King received the "Steady on" command, but failed to go straight toward the sheep. Instead he moved just a few steps around to the right of the sheep and then went straight toward them in order that he could bring them straight to me.

I knew something King didn't – the sheep had to travel to a gateway before they could come to me. When he made the decision to gather and drive the sheep according to his judgment rather than follow my direction exactly, he put the sheep in a difficult spot crowded up against the fence. All was not in vain, but it did mean that we had to stop where we were and proceed with a new beginning.

It is a common occurrence in working with a stock, or sheep dog; often are the times that a dog will make a slight alteration to the command he was given and therefore must be stopped. By far the most important and most often used command for the stock dog is "Sit." In essence it means whoa

– hold everything – let's settle down, regroup and start over! Nothing is worse than an untrained stock dog bent on exercising his ability to drive, bark, bite and cause all manner of havoc while completely ignoring everything the owner might shout at him. Training a dog to sit, or lie down with faithful obedience can be the beginning step for other useful instructions.

As soon as I saw the problem I gave King the "Sit" command, He was obedient. I allowed a few moments for everything to settle down. King relaxed and so did the sheep without the relentless pursuit by the dog. The next commands were given to gently move the sheep for a short distance to a gateway into the field where I stood.

How often do you think Christians, with knowledge of the Bible, and years of training and experience, get their minds set to do God's will in the same way King attempted to drive my sheep? History, from Biblical times to our present day, tells how many men earnestly followed God's clear directions for a while, and then at some point began to make slight alterations (doing it my way, right?) that led to problems.

Many cults seemed to have formed when men with a Biblical base gradually went their own way. Those who study aberrant teaching in churches find that some men have started with correct goals, but then began to make slight alterations. That's one way that something described as sin in the Bible is sometimes changed to fit man's modern definition such as alternate lifestyle, values clarification, situation ethics, and a woman's "right to choose" murder. Unfortunately we have decision makers at the top of entire church denominations that have made these mistakes.

How often does the Bible instruct us to remain in constant communication with God? We are instructed to meditate on His Word day and night, to be still before the Lord, and to pray without ceasing. Today's manna will not be good for tomorrow anymore than yesterday's manna will sustain us for today. Sometimes we may move steadily toward the goal as we perceive it and encounter huge problems. It may be plans for a career, a five-year professional goal, or simply plans for this day. Perhaps we need to sit. Can we be still long enough to receive through His Word, from our prayer time, and from godly counsel, directions that we know are "steps ordered by the Lord"?

28

Beyond the Breadbasket

*Then I heard the voice of the Lord saying,
'Whom shall I send?' (Isaiah. 6:8)*

January 1994. Sometime during my elementary school years I saw a map that made a lasting impression. I can still picture that map outlining the United States of America, but that was not the thing that made such an impression, one that I see clearly even now, more than 40 years later. It was a dark shaded area in the middle part of the map. The large shaded area of that map designated the Corn Belt. This region of the map was called "the breadbasket of the world," or at least that is how I remembered it all through the years. The great Midwest and its productive farmland was something for a young West Virginia boy to wonder about; it seemed like such a wonderful place, and such a long way from where I lived.

As I grew older and my interest in agriculture increased I was positively influenced by many people, particularly those in the 4-H programs in our state. Since the 4-H programs were an agricultural extension of the land grant universities, those working at such institutions also had a stimulating effect on my desire to study and work in agriculture.

My freshman year in the College of Agriculture at West Virginia University was like sitting at the feet of fired up evangelists. Several of the faculty in agriculture repeatedly told us that farmers in America could feed the world. It was an exciting time of my life, hearing over and over that American agriculture was the solution to the hunger throughout the world. I enjoyed the camaraderie with fellow students who caught the same vision, the vision to help feed the world by becoming a part of American agriculture.

As the years passed I continued my schooling getting degrees at three different land grant colleges. I also worked for the agricultural extension service in two of those states. During those years of study and work I continued to hear and tell the story about how the world could be fed through the efforts of American agriculturalists. At the time I was finishing my Ph.D. in Animal Science I decided that I would prefer to work in one of two geographic regions of the U.S., either the growing agricultural southeast or the well-established Midwest.

I thought I had died and gone to a heaven for agriculturalists after having worked a short while in northeast Missouri at the southern end of the Corn Belt that I had heard about since childhood. I found it difficult to believe one could turn on a television set and see advertisements for farm tractors, fertilizers and agricultural chemicals. It took some adapting to live in an environment where farming is Number One – I loved it!

What a delight to have young men and women from Midwest farms enter my classroom to study toward a career in agriculture. Farm boys and girls were leaving the farm to study agriculture, and then begin a farming career or become part of some other agricultural business to help feed the world. In a sense I was a product of my earlier training.

I had become somewhat of an evangelist for agriculture. One of the highest compliments ever paid to me at Northeast Missouri State University was by the Dean of instruction. Since he had been trained in the liberal arts, he and I were adversaries of sorts, but each of us had some respect for the other. One day as he introduced me to someone in his office, he said, "Dr. Rowan sells agriculture." My frequent trips to his office as an advocate for the agriculture program at NMSU prompted his remark.

But that was also about the time I realized, "Hey this isn't working!" We are not feeding the world. As a matter of fact no one is." I realized I was part of a system that had been operating for several decades. American farmers were becoming more productive and more efficient. In a sense it was a machine that developed a life all its own; young people were studying agriculture and becoming the next generation that would improve agricultural technology in the United States and then train the following generation to do the same. Fewer farmers were producing at a higher rate, but very little seemed to be accomplished toward helping Third World countries because we were not going beyond the breadbasket.

I realized I was doing nothing to influence others to directly help solve hunger in other parts of the world, and I began to see that one reason for my failure to do that was because no one had ever pointed me in that direction either. This period of my life coincided with a time I began to really discover God's Word, and the importance of trying to live by the Book.

That was the point where I began to see that it was not the responsibility of the American farmer to feed the world; it was not the responsibility of the farmers living and working in the "breadbasket of the world" to feed everyone on this earth. Likewise it was not the responsibility of the land grant colleges, American agricultural businesses, or any other institutions in agriculture to feed the hungry. I came to realize it is the responsibly of the Church, the Christian! Certainly Christians who also happen to be farmers are in a distinctive position to help feed the world, but the responsibility clearly rests with all Christians, and particularly those in positions of leadership.

Since leaving the college campus and returning to the farm where I was raised, I have spent much time during the past 10 years studying the Bible, the Church, church government, and ministries of different types, particularly those with a foreign mission emphasis. I have attempted to do this without loosing thought of the fact that much of the world is hungry for food to nourish the physical body, and an even greater number have a hunger that only Jesus Christ can satisfy.

Sometimes our quest for the truth reveals some disappointing facts. Here it is; we (Christians) will not **go beyond the breadbasket** until we **go beyond the church pew**! Until the Church looks beyond the comforts of hearing a nice message in a comfortable building on Sunday morning we will do little to be obedient to the instructions found in the Bible to carry the gospel beyond the church pew.

The American church has a cycle not unlike the one I perceived in American agriculture with one obvious difference; statistics show the American consumer has been a blessed benefactor of progress in agriculture in the form of high quality, low cost food. In contrast, the fruits shown by people's behavior in our society suggest that Christians are not making a difference in America. Even a casual look at national statistics revealing that churches in the U.S. spend 99% of our income on Christians says much about our misguided priorities.

But I have also found many Christians who want to follow Jesus' commands regardless of the pressures in our society. I have met several individuals and also learned of some organizations that see the need to **go beyond the breadbasket**, and they realize that they must first be committed to **go beyond**

the church pew. Who is willing to go, to go beyond the church pew and beyond the breadbasket? Could the words of the prophet Isaiah penned so long ago be appropriate now? "Then I heard the voice of the Lord saying, 'Whom shall I send? And who will go for us.'" And I said, "Here I am. Send me!" (Isaiah 6:8)

29

Sheep Following Sheep – Through the Fog

–the rulers gather together against the Lord and his Anointed One. (Psalm 2:2)

April 1994. It was a peaceful morning with a heavy fog hanging over the farm. I enjoyed the quiet walk out to a sheep pasture as I carried a bag of salt on my shoulder. My flock of sheep was still lying quietly as I walked past them to the place where I deposited their salt. Since it was still early in the morning and so peaceful I decided to climb on a large rock near the sheep and spend a few moments there.

My presence in the pasture apparently spurred the sheep to arise as they gradually did so, one by one. They then began to move, to walk so they could begin the morning grazing before the sun became so hot. Most of the flock walked single file within 50 feet of where I sat on the rock. They paid no attention to me, but rather seemed a bit like half asleep creatures just following the flow of those in the lead.

I was almost certain where the sheep were going, and it seemed a bit ridiculous. Yes, I found it a bit difficult to believe what I sensed they were doing. A few minutes later the whole flock of perhaps 250 sheep was standing in one corner of the field – not grazing, not going anywhere, not doing anything but standing near a gate.

I sensed early that the sheep were reacting to learned behavior that had carried over from the previous grazing season. The previous year the gateway between two pastures had been open throughout the entire grazing season, but I had changed management practices this particular year and I had shut the gate between the two grazing areas. I knew the sheep had been in this particular pasture for enough days to know the boundaries and the closed gateways, yet they arose from their beds and nonchalantly began walking toward the other pasture. It was sheep following sheep, through the fog, if I have ever seen it.

Each sheep was plodding along with its nose close to the tail of the sheep immediately in from of it, seemingly unaware of me, the shepherd, nearby. Although each and every sheep should have known the gate was closed, they seemed to give no thought to the direction they were headed, and then they were ultimately piled up in a corner with the entire exercise merely a demonstration of futile activity. I thought to myself, "That describes Christianity in America during the last half of the 20th Century if anything does–sheep following sheep, through the fog."

I often wonder why we Christians do what we do, and in many cases why we tolerate much of what is happening in our society. Why does it seem such a mystery that our nation has so many problems? A better question is, "Why are we doing so little to turn the tide toward the Gospel?"

Why are we Christians not on our face before God seeking his direction when we see and hear the leaders of such high position in our land speak openly about the need to teach our young school children how to use condoms as a precaution for safe sex? "Are they ashamed of their loathsome conduct? No, they have no shame at all; they do not even know how to blush." (Jer. 6:15) Why does this not infuriate us? Why do we take it so lightly? Why do we not vomit when we see such leaders on television programs broadcast across the nation? Why do we just hang our head low with our nose just inches from the dirty rear end of the sheep in front of us?

A few days ago I heard a psychologist on TV say that our children need to be taught how to be mothers because our children are having children and don't know how to take care of them. So what is so mysterious about such a thing as motherhood? We don't need another government program aimed at a problem we Christians should know cannot be solved by civil governments of any kind. We must stop looking to the government as the answer for every problem that comes along. A civil government "gathered against the Lord and his Anointed One" cannot provide solutions to spiritual problems!

We have been in the pasture long enough to know that some gates are no longer open. Let's get our heads out of the fog! For example, we need Christian leaders in public school systems, but we need to quit following such systems. Instead, church congregations, under the lead of the Holy Spirit, need to set the standards. When will church congregations begin to support Christian schools, or start their own schools? Is following others to a virtual dead end in the corner of a field the best we Christians can do?

What are we Christians doing about the welfare of others? What are we doing about the financial security of the disabled, the aged, and the genuinely poverty stricken? What about health care? Do we Christians think health care can only be obtained by the payment of an insurance premium and/or provided by some civil government? Have we

Christians sought the Bible for answers to any/all of these, or have we just followed the flow of those in the lead?

Never before in our nation's history have we had set before us a group of leaders that so accurately fit the description in Psalm 2:2. Never before have we had people in the highest courts in the land, the highest legislative body, and particularly the highest executive branch of the United States of America who have so openly "gathered together against the Lord and against his Anointed One."

Permanently etched in concrete throughout our nation's capital are Scriptures and phrases that bare testimony to this country's founding Christian fathers. Thank God for them, but now the Scriptures speak, "How long, O men will you turn my glory into shame? How long will you love delusions and seek false gods?" (Psalm 4:2)

Who do you and I follow? Do we follow the Lord and his Anointed One, or do we follow those who have not been "born again," those who lack spiritual discernment, those who are plodding along through the fog on a dead end trail?

With Psalm 2 we began, with Psalm 2 we end; "Kiss the Son, lest he be angry and you be destroyed in your way, for his wrath can flare up in a moment. Blessed are all who take refuge in him." (Psalm 2:12)

30

The Other Side of the Fence

He who walks with the wise grows wise, but companion of fools suffers harm. (Proverbs 13:20)

1994. No, you are not going to read about how the grass is greener on the other side of the fence. That's old hat because most everyone is aware of the expression even though they may not appreciate how man (a livestock farmer, no doubt) coined that phrase. Besides, there is something far more tempting than the grass on the other side of the fence. You read correctly, there is something more tempting than the grass in the other pasture. Knowing the behavior of farm animals I'm convinced that sheep teach this best of all.

Let's take a look at fences. There are barrier fences and psychological fences. Barrier fences properly constructed and maintained provide a literal barrier that sheep cannot penetrate through, go under or over. Woven wire, rails, boards and multi-stranded barbed wire can provide such a barrier. A "psychological fence" (you may not want to repeat that – I'm not sure it has common usage) is electrified. If an animal's first few encounters with the fence provide a good shock then the beast learns some respect for the fence and will seldom challenge it even though a quick bolt through the parallel wires would be fairly simple and relatively harmless because the fence does not provide a physical barrier. We have constructed a lot of this electric fence at Psalm 23 and realize the psychological effects of this fence are great until a sheep is really tempted to go to the other side. Do you know what's more tempting on the other side than green grass? It's other sheep. That's right, sheep on the other side of the fence.

People have gregarious behavior or the instinct to flock together the same as sheep. Oh, we think we are so independent, but how lonely would it be if you and I went 24 hours without the sound of another human voice or sight of another person. Chances are most who read this never have had such an experience. I never have. Teens are much more susceptible to gregarious behavior, peer pressures, and adapting group values than are adults. There is no doubt in my mind teen-agers would rather be with a group of their own age studying the Bible than being in a theater watching an X rated, R rated, or PG 13 rated movie (all translate into un-godly entertainment) all alone, or with their parents. You already know teens want to do what "everybody" is doing. (everybody, of course, means some others of their own age.) People don't watch dirty movies, listen to vulgar rock songs, drink alcohol, shoot drugs, and live recklessly because it looks greener over there; it's because other sheep are over there. By the way, sheep are more apt to go through the electric fence to join others they recognize as a part of their flock than they are to go join the neighbor's flock.

Many years ago I heard my Mother explain how the correct way to deal with a baby or small child was to substitute (e.g. trade the sharp knife the baby has for a rubber ball). My former co-worker, Dr. Bob Stone, Professor of Agricultural Economics, taught me a lesson years ago about students and cheating – remove the temptation. The best of students put under pressure with temptation in front of them may peek at their neighbor's test paper, but not if his closest neighbor is too far away. Bob Stone put distance between his students during an exam. If I really want to avoid mixing sub flocks of my sheep I avoid placing them in adjoining pastures unless there's a barrier fence between them.

We let the world baby sit our children via the TV. We let the world educate our children, (public schools without God) and we let the world entertain them, set their priorities and establish their value system. Then we don't understand why they act the way they do. After all, they go to church two hours every week! Christian people, the psychological fences we build for our growing flock are no better than the way we hold the flock together on this side of the fence or the distance we put between our flock and the other sheep. Here at Psalm 23 my standard shepherding practice is to place sheep, especially lambs (more apt to join the neighbors flock) two pastures away from the next group of sheep (removing temptation). No, green grass is not the greatest temptation; it's the other sheep.

When Jesus told Peter, "Feed my lambs." (John 21:15), He no doubt meant for him to properly tend to the spiritual needs of the young people. Perhaps we need some substitutions on this side of the fence to keep our flock in the right pasture while luring more lost ones to our side of the fence. Pray about it, read your Bible, pray again, and then put some feet to your prayers.

31

One Lame Sheep After Another

Be sure you know the condition of your flocks, give careful attention to your herds. (Proverbs 27:23)

January 1995. It was disastrous! How could it have happened right before my eyes? There must have been between 30 and 40 percent of my flock with a disease called foot rot.

It all began one summer when I noticed a lame sheep in my flock. Lameness is common among sheep as their feet are easily injured and also very vulnerable to certain infections, so I do not become alarmed when I see a single lame sheep. However, this particular summer was different; we had a big problem. The problem was my negligence, because the single sheep was joined by a second lame sheep; then there was a third, a fourth, etc. until finally a few months later I seemed to have awakened to the fact that I had a large number of sheep with foot rot, a very serious disease.

I had heard about the dreaded foot rot disease for more than forty years but had never had a first hand experience with an infected flock. I learned from a veterinarian several years ago that foot rot can develop in any lame sheep if conditions are right. A successful shepherd had once told me that once the flock is infected the disease will always be there, but it is easy to be kept in check with prompt treatment to any new lame sheep. If the disease goes unchecked a massive problem will surely inhabit the flock. So there I was with a flock where one lame sheep after another added up to a big, big problem; and it could have been prevented!

So goes the American culture, one lame sheep after another, leading to the deplorable condition we now have. Only God knows about the first lame sheep, but make no mistake about it, America has had many signs over time that should have alerted us to the impending decline in our country. No attempt is made here to give exhaustive details of lame sheep signs in American culture, but rather to focus on three, and to show some association. In other words, does one lame sheep help infect another?

Lame Sheep No. 1 - Excellence to mediocrity. A healthy people strive for excellence. In his letter to the Colossians Paul wrote "Whatever you do, work at it with all your heart, as working for the Lord, not for men." (Col 3:23) Christians are admonished to strive for excellence; how else can we interpret this scripture? I have seen in my lifetime a decline in attitudes towards striving for excellence. In fact, many students will readily tell you that they hesitate to excel because their peers may ostracize them.

The first time I saw clearly the lame sheep of mediocrity replacing excellence was in 1966 as a new county agricultural agent in North Carolina. Part of my duties involved work with the 4-H Club program in one of the mountain counties. I had just completed six years of college training and had worked hard to that end. A few months after beginning work there the county-wide 4-H program held an awards program, or Achievement Night, as it was called. It was my duty to determine who was to receive awards. That was fine, all I needed was to see project records and evaluate them. Having had 12 years experience as a 4-H Club member in West Virginia, I welcomed the chance to work in this new capacity.

Here was the situation on past awards in that program. Members were not required to complete their 4-H projects in order to receive an award; they only needed to be listed as an enrolled member. I was not used to such rewarding of individuals for their effortlessness. I had no real problems in trying to institute some reform, but I thought it was interesting that an official from the state office once told me in a private conference that it was important for me to understand that for the sake of the young people we should reward them for just being on the roll. I did not buy that idea then, and I don't buy that idea now, nearly 20 years later.

Approximately five years later I began teaching in a college and was very disturbed to see a similar trend where excellence in individual effort was changing to the lame sheep of mediocrity. During a committee meeting with faculty from across the campus one math professor in the group said he figured that any student who signed up for his course was entitled to at least a C grade. Later I learned that that attitude prevailed among many faculty members. So, enrolling was worth a C and if the student was a good ole boy, then perhaps he should have a B. Some were convinced that long-term, perhaps permanent damage would come to individuals who received even one low grade. My biggest disappointment was my inability to find very many people who agreed that this was a trend that would some day prove disastrous. People in leadership refused to accept it, and others were afraid to speak up. Now, many years later we have a generation raised as lame sheep of mediocrity. The decline in standard test scores has proved that, and unfortunately many of today's schoolteachers are products of that lame sheep of mediocrity. The latest move in the "dumbing down" of America is that companies that produce standardized tests will lower their standards. Everyone wants a high score, right?

Lame Sheep No. 2- God to Government. What ever happened to "In God We Trust" and "The Lord Is My Shepherd?" We have become a people who have become increasingly dependant upon the government as our provider. Of course it should not be surprising since the lame sheep of mediocrity produced a people who want to receive something without working for it.

Many people point to the time when prayer was taken out of public schools as a turning point where God began to be pushed out of our society, particularly anything having to do with agencies supported by our government. It may not have been the first, but it was certainly a significant lame sheep moment in American history. The sign was there, we saw it, but ignored it and went on our merry way – just like my sheep during early stages when the disease was slowly spreading throughout my flock.

It is the job of the church to put God first and bring converts to Christianity, so the primary blame for any lameness whereby government replaces God lies with Christians. This is particularly true in the USA where historical records accurately show that we did begin as a Christian nation. You are well aware of the progressively blatant hostility toward Christianity that has evolved in recent years. Much of that stems from the fact that we looked to and believed corrupt government(s) when in fact we should have kept our eyes on God. Give attention to what the Bible says about corruptness in high places. "Can a corrupt throne be allied with you – one that brings on misery by its decrees? They band together against the righteous and condemn the innocent to death." (Psalm 94:20-21) – condemn the innocent to death? Read on!

Lame Sheep No. 3 - Life to Death. We began as One Nation Under God, and now we are plagued by the ideology of multiculturalism that has pitted one social class against another. It seems each class believes the others have victimized it. Or, as some have promoted the idea that all problems are due to middle-aged, white males of European ancestry. It seems that every time you turn around there is another group of people who wants special "rights." It's the "in thing" to claim your rights have been violated, and therefore you can demand special treatment.

This selfish attitude has infested individuals as well as groups promoting the idea that "my life and what I want is of paramount importance and no one else counts for anything." It is no longer "You and me babe." Instead, it's "Me, but not you babe!" Twice during the past week I heard concerned individuals on radio and TV make the comment that went something like this, "Our kids really don't know right from wrong behavior."

Here's an example: if someone has a pair of shoes that you like, then take a gun, shoot him, and just take his shoes. I realize a crime such as this is extreme and does not happen on every street corner, or in every city, but it does occur. This type behavior is rooted in selfishness and a total disregard for the sanctity of life. It is a product of our lame sheep attitude about the value of the life on this earth that God gave to all of us.

A pro-life movement should be unthinkable in our country. Everyone should be for life without having a special movement and special organization that seeks to preserve life. It should not be a part of our thinking that we would consider anything else. Why even consider the intentional murder of an innocent unborn baby? The very words pro choice indicate the selfishness of what I call the pro-death group. Many people say they are not for abortion, but they are for the rights of a woman to choose what she does with her body. If I am pro-choice then I am, in fact, pro-death because it means I approve of an individual's decision to commit murder. It doesn't help society when our government promotes the idea of condemning the innocent to death.

Suppose a mother decides for whatever reason that she no longer wants her two young children. Would she be considered a pro-choicer and therefore be allowed by our society to drown her children if she chooses?

The point of this article is not to simply identify lame sheep symptoms in our society. We should have a consensus by now that our country has problems. We missed the warning signs many years ago, but like the example with my sheep we failed to act upon what we saw. Simply, but accurately put, we should heed Proverbs 27:23, "Be sure you know the condition of your flocks, give careful attention to your herds."

32

Yearlings Unattended and the Second Reading of the Law

These commandments that I give you today are to be upon your heart. Impress them on your children. Talk about them when you sit at home and when you walk along the road, when you lie down and when you get up.
(Deuteronomy 6:6:7)

Winter 1996. For a number of years I was very careful to see that my yearling sheep received proper direction. I was careful because I know that the pattern set at this point in their life has important bearing on how they act in the future. Sheep that are two years and older can be trusted. They know the boundaries and generally stay within them. My careful watch in rearing yearlings and my quickness to train them in the way they should go does much to shape a flock that conforms to my wishes. Incidentally, I don't train lambs; they follow their mothers.

I then had a period of about three years where I exercised little control over the flock. At the end of that three-year period I had a very different flock. Since sheep have such a short life, the two and three year olds usually have major influence over the entire flock; they do most of the leading. They are also a bit bossy over the younger and the older sheep.

It was a bit discouraging when I woke up to what had happened, because I suddenly realized these were not the type sheep I thought I had. I had neglected to give them proper direction and they in large part were selecting their own paths to travel.

This experience showed me clearly that our American culture has gone the way of the unattended yearling. Who has been giving direction to our youth, the young adults, the impressionable, during the past two or three generations?

Consider the degeneration in our culture We have an increase in single parent families, illegitimate children, abuse of spouses and children, the move away from small community influence, a decreased influence of the local church over people's lifestyles, the increase in sexual perversion, and the decrease in the value of life as evidenced by violent crime and the intentional abortion of babies. What happened?

Most Christian would agree that America needs a spiritual renewal. Most Christians agree that we are, as individuals, responsible for our behavior, but we also know that other people can have a tremendous influence on our lives. This is especially true with our young people. They, like the yearlings, given proper direction will follow older people but left unattended will forge a path of their own.

"He leadeth me in paths of righteousness for his name's sake." (Ps 23:3, KJV) Have we been following God during the past 30 to 40 years? Has there been some type of unified effort or goal or set of godly standards that the masses have focused on during this time. I say, "No."

Sheep Tracks

As a child growing up in this rural community there were hardly any distinctions made between school, church, community organizations, and youth groups. Two ministers taught in our school. Each spring while in grade school we had a weeklong Bible school in public school. Can you imagine that now? You might say we didn't know too much about what was wrong in society because we seemed to be continually exposed to what was correct; at least that is my impression. I don't mean that the adults who lived their lives before us were perfect, but there were certain things considered unacceptable in our society and therefore we seldom saw such behavior.

Let me give one example. Sex or pregnancy, without benefit of marriage, was a no, no! It should be today, but instead we reward it. Now we give the unwed mother money, food, and special housing and dare the pregnant teen's family, church and community to say the girl and the baby's father have done anything wrong.

A few days ago I heard someone say with respect to having Bill Clinton elected President of the United States of America, "We got what we asked for!" Amen to that! Regardless of your political inclination you will likely agree that Bill Clinton is not our problem; he merely mirrors much of our present culture. More accurately, he represents and leads a rebellious group that went their own way as "yearlings." Spring shearing improves the looks of my wayward sheep, but it doesn't change their attitude. The same can be said of many of the 60's "flower children."

Remember, the new crop of adult sheep is aggressive toward the young and the old. Many young and old people are vulnerable to lies and other deceitful tactics of those in leadership positions.

Our Christianity has been fragmented to the extent that one's religion and one's relationship to work, play and community tends to be segregated, and each aspect of our life is put in a different pigeonhole, so to speak. When

Christianity ceased to be central to our community and our lives, we lost our way.

In contrast to the type community in which I was raised, Christians and the Christian lifestyle are now sources of ridicule and many forms of rejection by community, government, and even by some so-called churches. Now we have a nation not of one people, but one of many cultures, sub-cultures, and counter-cultures, each attempting to go its own way.

Who is leading the flock? The book of Deuteronomy is a good source of comfort and direction for me. The word "Deuteronomy" is derived from two Greek works, *deuteros*, meaning "second" and *nomos*, "law." God had a rebellious generation of Israelites that had to remain in the wilderness until they died, and it became necessary for the new generation to have the law repeated before they could enter the Promised Land. That seems to be our position now. We've wondered in the wilderness, gone our own way and now constitute a totally different flock. With my flock of sheep, it is very difficult to retrain a wayward group of sheep. It works much better to start with the young and carefully train them.

The prognosis? It's time for the "second reading of the law." A whole new generation of young Christians have the literal opportunity of a lifetime! I'm reminded of the story of the two shoe salesmen who went to a primitive section of Africa. One returned dejected saying he couldn't sell shoes there because the people don't wear shoes. The second salesman returned bubbling with enthusiasm as he related to his sales manager, "What a fantastic marketing opportunity, no one there has any shoes!"

Young Christians can take the attitude of the optimistic shoe salesman and dedicate themselves to living by God's Word. They have such clear cut opportunity and challenge like no other group of people on earth! They of course, can't do this unattended. Will you help them?

33

The Best Tasting Water in the World

–to him who is thirsty I will give to drink without cost from the spring of the water of life. (Revelation 21:6)

August 1998. Early this morning I hiked up Peter's Mountain to a spring that my grandfather developed as a source of piped water into his home almost 80 years ago. After several weeks without significant rainfall I visited the spring to check the volume at the overflow pipe. I found the output of that spring to be considerably less than any time I had checked it in the past, no doubt a result of dry weather and heavy use. The spring serves our farm, the farm belonging to my cousin who owns the spring, and a water bottling company that uses several thousand gallons each day.

Three times during recent years the water from that spring has been entered in international competition. A panel of judges has three times judged it "the best tasting water in the world." Our families drank that wonderful water for many decades without knowing its value although we were aware that it was way ahead of the water our city cousins had in their homes.

As I studied the flow I began to think about the visit my wife Glenda, our son Mark and I had to Israel last winter. The Jordan River is nearly dry as it enters the Dead Sea because so much is taken from it for irrigation purposes. Our tour guide told us that the next war in the Middle East will be for water. He said it is not whether, but just a matter of when.

It seems as though our Christian culture in America is much like the spring with a reduced flow, or like a valuable river that becomes depleted. There is no mystery about the value of water in this life, but for Christians we have no worries about the after life because the Bible has given that description, "– drink without cost from the spring of the water of life." The Christian culture may seem to be declining in numbers, but we still have **the best tasting water out of this world.**

34

Feeding and Protecting Our Lambs

– let them rule over the fish of the sea and the birds of the air, over the livestock, over all the earth, and over all the creatures that move along the ground. (Genesis: 1:26)

September 1998. During a period of two or three years young lambs in my sheep flock were dying at an increasing rate. It happened each spring in our pasture lambing management program. I would often find the carcass of a lamb up to a month of age that had been picked over by vultures. I wrongly concluded the lambs were dying from a lack of nutrition or perhaps some disease. I finally learned that coyotes were killing lambs during the night or early morning hours and the vultures were simply getting the left-overs. Coyotes had moved into our geographic area without my knowledge.

Initially I felt a lot of frustration because we soon learned that the coyote is very sly and elusive with the ability to be a problem in spite of man's efforts. Realizing God's Word says we have dominion over all living creatures I knew a solution was not impossible.

Our culture in America is rapidly skidding downward; it is no longer a debatable issue. Like the slaughter of my lambs, our first step is to realize we have a problem. Second, we must identify the enemy (Satan). Third, we must know the One who holds the answers. Fourth, we must take steps to change management.

I do not compare our children to the sheep in the sense of a literal physical slaughtering of our young people; it is spiritual matters that are salient here. I will hasten to say that one could write much about the "slaughter of the lambs" in reference to our children. It could be abortion, drugs, teens killing teens with weapons, and other examples as well.

Now, what about our "lambs," our children? Are they in more danger now than children were 40 to 50 years ago from a spiritual standpoint? I think so. As I see it, the main challenge Christians have in this culture is that of understanding that we cannot reason with unbelievers using biblical principles. Our culture is post-Christian, so there is little likelihood any serious dialog can take place between the two groups.

Why is it near impossible to reason with unbelievers? The Bible says, "The man without the Spirit does not accept the things that come from the Spirit of God, for they are foolishness to him, and he cannot understand them, because they are spiritually discerned." (1 Cor. 2:14) This explains why we have such heated debates about issues such as abortion and homosexuality.

Review the steps:

1. There's a problem,
2. There's an enemy,
3. There is a source for the answer, and
4. Management must change.

Step 1. Believers and non-believers alike will agree we have a problem. However, agreement between the group ends right here.

Step 2. Satan is our enemy. As long as I was unaware that coyotes were killing my lambs, I was not about to get a clue as to how the slaughter could be stopped. Vaccinating lambs would not help. Drenching my lambs with worming compounds was not a solution. If Christians understand that Satan is orchestrating our problems then we have a place to begin working toward solutions. However, I don't advise you to go to government offices in Washington, D.C. or show up at a local school board meeting to preach to them about how we need to handle Satan.

Step 3. God is our source. Our founding fathers knew this. Our current "fathers" do not. Enough said!

Step 4. Management change. If we believe and understand numbers one, two and three, then step four is easier to implement.

When I finally realized the enemy was the coyote, then I made efforts to learn more about this predator. It is a very rare occasion when I see a coyote. However, I do know that I must understand the habits of both the coyote and the sheep in order to protect my lambs.

Children are like lambs. We need to understand children, know the tactics of their enemy, and then begin to set new management in place. Public education is the number one target for management change. Why? Children spend five days a week there – like young lambs on spring pasture, they are easy targets. I suspect that many people reading this never heard of *"Its Elementary,"* a film produced by homosexuals and being placed in public schools across America.

It is a "warm fuzzy" presentation about the supposed merits of homosexual behavior.

This pro-homosexual film probably doesn't describe anal sex and blood letting that causes the transmission of HIV. I doubt that the film tells about the real dangers of homosexuality that take an average of 30 years off the life of men. These same people try to tell your children and grandchildren that homosexuals were born that way. They call their behavior "orientation" and natural, and you are a right wing homophobe if you call it perversion. The fact is many homosexuals are predators with the slyness of the coyote at entering the sheep pen, so to speak, looking for young lambs.

As a young boy I would occasionally hear about someone in a car accident that "totaled" the car. I thought that meant that the car was so damaged that not a single part could be used. Of course I later learned that there could be many good parts, but it would be less expensive to go buy another car just like the one wrecked than it would be to repair the one in the crash.

My friend, on a nationwide basis, public schools are like a totaled automobile; there are lots of good people, staff, teachers, administrators, and students left in these schools. However it is time for Christians to get a replacement, one school at a time, because the old system is totaled. The 1957 happy days model is a fond memory but not a present day reality.

I remember the time when informed people denied that we had a problem in our schools. I saw about 25 years pass before most people quit denying it. Of course it's hard to deny when kids are gunning other kids down right on school property. Now its time to change management, but I suspect another 25 years may pass before Christians realize they need to provide that five-day a week environment that is different from the one presently controlled by those with a very different agenda. Who do you think should manage our kids for that five-day period each week?

35

Clean Pasture

Is it not enough for you to feed on the good pasture? Must you also trample the rest of your pasture with your feet? Must my flock feed on what you have trampled and drink what you have muddied with your feet?
(Ezekiel 34:18-19)

November 1999. What is clean pasture? In the animal industry it has a specific definition for some of us. Clean pasture for my sheep is one void of contamination from parasitic worms, larvae and/or eggs. Specifically for our sheep, a clean pasture is one that has had no other sheep on it for a period of at least 12 months. It may be relatively clean with a rest of three, six or eight months, but not truly clean like a 12-month period would give.

A contaminated pasture is very harmful to lambs as they are very susceptible to such parasites. Older animals develop some immunity and therefore have at least moderate protection from these microscopic parasites. For the shepherd who wants to give his lambs the best, he will reserve designated portions of the grazing lands each year for his weaned lambs. The shepherd will not let his lambs be exposed to any contaminated pasture (any pasture that has had sheep on it during the past year) until they become relatively mature.

Mother, father, grandparent, friend, and student, what do you think the environment is like in America's public, state controlled schools here at the close of the Twentieth Century? Are they as clean as a good shepherd's pasture? Of course they are not! They are absolutely filthy! There is no reason for me to give an exhaustive account of things that have happened in recent years that proves my point about the degenerate condition of public schools. However, as long as we have deplorable schools some of us feel compelled to make suggestions for making change.

One of the deceptive things about sheep pasture is that there are times when the pasture looks beautiful, but in reality it is heavily contaminated. For example, ample rainfall on a pasture that has been fertilized with manure while being heavily grazed will bring forth a beautiful dark green grass. As good as it looks it is usually heavily contaminated with parasites. So what are the analogies with public schools?

Let's take a look. Public schools look good because we are paying for them anyway, and they have the following: some nice buildings, an organizational structure in place, a lot of variety in the curriculum, sports programs, plus other extra curricular programs that seem to be attractive to many parents and students. Poppycock! It is like the dark green grass in a contaminated pasture field! Beneath the lush green is a subtle insidious contamination that must surely grieve our Holy God.

Christians are familiar with Proverbs 22:6 commanding us to "Train up a child in the way he should go." Are there Christians who honestly believe public schools make a contribution to this commandment? The jury is not in session on the value of public schools. The verdict is in; public schools have failed. Some people point to the fact that their child goes to a good public school or that the child's teacher is a Christian. That is great on the surface, but when considering our entire country and occasional good school or Christian teacher is like a single clean bite of grass in a 100-acre pasture field. Motivational speaker Zig Zigler says you can occasionally find a good biscuit in a garbage can, but it is no place to go looking for one. Ditto for public schools! I just think we should be smart enough to dismount our horse after he has been dead so long he stinks.

If I grazed my lambs on contaminated pasture five days a week, then placed them in clean pasture two days a week, and follow this with another five-day period on a parasite infested pasture any knowledgeable shepherd would call me foolish for such a practice.

Clean pasture, how does the lamb get it? The mother ewe doesn't provide it, the shepherd does. Is it difficult? Yes, it takes time, planning and a lot of work. Who is responsible for a child's training? It is obviously not the child. Not so easy is getting adult Christians to realize that it is not the responsibility of any civil government either. On an individual basis, the family, the parents are responsible. On a secondary level the Church or local church congregations are responsible. And here is where the ax really falls; it is the leadership in the church, the pastor, who must accept the major responsibility.

If a man says he is called by God to pastor a church congregation in 1999 in the USA and is not making a concerted effort in the pulpit to direct his flock to clean pasture (getting the lambs out of public schools) then I, without hesitation, say he is missing part of his calling!

Two dozen church programs designed to bring more people in the front door of a church can do little at raising young lambs compared with 3-6 hours a day of Christ centered training that can take place in a Christian home or within the walls of a Christian school. Discipleship, that's what it is, and who will claim that Jesus would recommend we put 5 to18 year-olds in America's public schools five days a week for training to become His disciple?

Pastors often proclaim themselves shepherd of a flock (their church congregation.) Most cater to the sheep with the heavy fleeces. In other words, pastors seek to satisfy the adults because it's the adults who pay the bills including the pastor's salary. Exaggerated and oversimplified? Perhaps, but no doubt accurate enough to make the point. It is not uncommon to find Sunday morning worshipers sitting in a million dollar building, and come Monday morning the kids are sitting in a public school because in the words of the pastor, "it costs too much" to have a Christian school. I wonder; does "it cost too much" spoken by leaders of prosperous church congregations fit in with "having a form of godliness but denying its power"? (2 Tim. 3:5) Isn't it amazing how people can believe God can perform miracles, but fail to believe God will guide a pastor and congregation toward schooling their children, giving them clean pasture?

God has some clear warning for adults, especially shepherds who fail to properly guide their sheep. "Woe to the shepherd of Israel who only take care of themselves – you eat the curds, clothe yourselves with the wool and slaughter the choice animals, but you do not take care of the flock." (Eze. 34:2-3)

36

Closed Herd

Therefore come out from them and be separate, says the Lord. Touch no unclean thing and I will receive you.
(2 Corinthians 6:17)

November 1999. The sheep herd at Psalm 23 Camp has been closed for a number of years. A closed herd means that no outside sheep have been introduced into the flock. The herd has been closed to new females for 15 years and closed to new males for about half that time. A closed herd can have its problems, but I shall concentrate on the good things.

During 1982, '83 and '84 we purchased more than 200 ewes with which to build our flock. For several years we must have had every sheep disease between here and eastern Colorado. We vaccinated and doctored for everything going it seems. Through careful selection, management and a great deal of perseverance I have witnessed the evolution of the type herd I had envisioned, not complete, but going in that direction.

Adaptation to the environment was central to the changes in my flock. In other words the sheep that reside here now do well with the type grazing lands, the temperatures, the rainfall, the topography, the type diseases prevalent, and the type care we give (or don't give). I had to make some hard choices that eliminated some sheep that would otherwise likely reproduced a "like kind," thus perpetuating the characteristics I did not like with that sheep.

Folks, that's where we are in 1999. The Scripture shown above has probably never been more relevant. When God says, "Come out from them and be separate" most of us cringe a bit wondering about what "goodies" we might have to forfeit if we are obedient to that command. Besides, have you noticed that people don't like to be told what they can't have? For that matter we don't really like to be told to do anything. Most of the mistakes we make today as Christians are centered on our efforts to play our game using their (the world's) playing field. Sorry it ain't gonna happen. It's not your best use of time trying to get NBC, ABC, CNN, and CBS to tell your Christian story.

It's not your best use of time trying to get elected officials in Washington to sponsor your "Christian bill." It's not your best use of time going to the local PTA meeting with thoughts of getting your Christian influence to make a difference in what the local public school is teaching your child. Notice that I did not say it is a "waste of time" to do those things. That type of Christian activism is okay but should not be top priority in the body of Christ.

If I had kept all the weak sheep trying to build a strong herd, it would have been fruitless in the end. My methods took many years of building. People don't want to work with long-range goals because it takes too much sacrifice, too much time without seeing results. It takes some vision to understand that separating ourselves from a fallen world while we surrender all to Christ is necessary in order to build His Church. You can't give it the Microsoft touch via the click of a computer mouse to give you a roll down menu showing the answers to life's challenges. For example you can fire off e-mail to your Senators until Jesus comes and it will not do what time spent working toward getting Christians to take their children out of public schools and put them in Christian schools or school them at home. There are Kingdom of God principles that require planting and watering while God provides the growth. It takes perseverance; it takes time, usually a long time. It may take generations of people. Furthermore our efforts to influence politicians, for example, is like trying to repair the top stories of a tall building when in fact, it is the foundation that is crumbling.

Like my closed herd, it is time a faithful remnant of Christians separate ourselves to rebuild America's Christian culture with God's biblical principles, and in time He can use us (or our grandchildren) to disciple the world.

37

A New Working Chute

Jesus said to his disciples, "If anyone would come after me, he must deny himself and take up his cross and follow me."
(Matthew 16:24)

December 2000. Our sheep-working chute is the most important facility here at our sheep operation because it is the place where each individual animal is observed and treated or ministered to. For approximately 17 years I used the facility I had built for working the sheep. It was a good but not an excellent working chute.

As I worked the sheep for all those years I began, through experience, to get ideas about how the facility could be improved. However, year after year I put up with the inefficiency, the bottle necks created by crowding sheep, the constant struggles trying to catch and treat each sheep until finally I took the time to tear out much of the old facility and renovate it in an effort to make it conform to my needs and the natural behavior of sheep when they enter the working area.

One of the keys to working sheep in such a facility is to know the behavior of the animals and then design it so it conforms to the choices they prefer to make. For example, sheep follow other sheep, so it is most helpful if each sheep entering the chute can see another sheep in front of it. Also they like well-lighted areas, hesitating if they cannot clearly see what is ahead. Problems arise too, such as crowding when two or more attempt to enter a space that is only large enough for one. It is ironic that they don't want to be first, they always want to follow another, but on the other hand, once one takes the lead, invariably many others then immediately rush to follow. We are not unlike sheep. I think of how teens, in particular, wait for another to take the lead, but then if some go they all want to go, and do it NOW.

Since the Bible makes so many references to sheep and shepherds and how we are like sheep, I seldom deal with major changes with my sheep flock that I don't think of how this may relate to our life as Christians. Let me set the stage for how I see my sheep working chute as a shadow of Christians and their behavior. I give two examples.

The first example is when Jesus Christ is considered as our shepherd. In this case I see our role as Christians as having the desire to conform to group behavior because of the gregarious, or flocking instincts that we have, but we must also, one by one, come to the Shepherd to have the Holy Spirit minister to us. In other words we can participate in a lot of group activities, worship, etc., but being a Christian comes only when each of us accepts and submits to Jesus Christ as Savior and Lord of our life.

A second way the sheep, shepherd and working chute can relate to our Christian life is that any who minister the gospel can be considered a shepherd. As pastors or others minister, the mechanics of properly gathering people can be important. Perhaps unlike herding through a sheep working chute, but nonetheless being aware of human behavior can be an important aspect of successful ministry.

Sheep Tracks

Back to my working chute. My new chute is a tremendous improvement over the old one. Most every problem I experienced with the old has now been solved; the sheep move smoothly and seldom cause problems. So why did I not make the changes earlier? Well, a primary reason is that I did not know if the new design would work until I actually built and tried the new chute. In other words, there was some risk involved. Suppose I went to the trouble and expense to build a new chute only to find out that it changed nothing with regard to working my sheep. Or worse, perhaps the new chute would be less desirable than the old one. The new one worked better than the old, and I am thankful for that. However, that uncertainty, that risk factor, prevented me from making the change many years ago.

Now lets consider sheep, shepherds, and working chutes as they relate to ministry, as we know it in the present day church. What do you think? Can we do better? Of course we can. As we look at our American culture, we can conclude that the USA is in a post-Christian culture. No longer do the masses look to the Church for direction. It is regrettable, but true. Why is this the case? I don't pretend to know, but suffice to say that many factors are likely involved. However, let's consider briefly the behavior of sheep, or in this case the behavior of people.

I suspect many don't follow the Church, because they don't see Christianity as relevant to their life. I will use music as an example. A study of church history shows that music has always been important in our culture and that churches have problems when they ignore it. In other words, if the church music is too far from what the world culture accepts, then people are slow to be attracted to the church. Sometimes the church seems to get hung up in a time warp something like a hundred years ago. Great music a hundred years ago may not be considered great today. Does Christianity hang on to 100-year old music, or is it religion that makes us hang on to 100-year old music? I don't suggest that we throw out all tradition in trying to attract sheep, but maybe churches should take a few risks to redesign our working chutes, as it were.

If we are to minister effectively should we not be aware of the current behavior of the sheep we wish to reach? One definition of insanity is "doing the same thing over and over again and expecting different results." For 17 years I used the same chute running thousands of sheep through, and basically I obtained the same results. I obtained different, and positive, results only after I made changes. Our culture needs the Christian influence, and lost people need Jesus, The Great, The Good, and The Chief Shepherd. Considering the degradation we've seen in American culture making some changes in how we minister may be a risk worth taking.

38

Under-shepherd Gets Kicked in the Head

It will be good for those servants whose master finds them watching when he comes. (Luke 12:37)

October 2001. Sport is our three-year old sheep-herding dog. He is my under-shepherd and quite valuable anytime I wish to move my flock. One morning in early September of this year he took a tremendous kick on the head from a donkey we keep with our sheep flock. The donkey is to protect against predators, and on that morning the under-shepherd just got too close to the donkey.

By the very nature of the way our sheep flock is managed it is often necessary that the dog and the donkey come in direct contact because each has a purpose. One is there all the time to protect the flock, and the other is there anytime I am working with the flock and need him to help herd the sheep. I had expected that something like this kick in the head might happen some day.

When Sport received the blow to the head I anticipated serious trouble because he could not stand or walk for more than a few moments at a time. I moved him into the shade of a large tree and began to think how I could go get a pickup truck a half mile away and come back to get him so he could be taken to a veterinarian. The good part of the story is that after a few minutes in the shade, Sport recovered enough to walk back to his kennel. I let him rest for a couple days before working him again. Now after a few weeks have passed, he seems to be fine. More importantly he seems to be more alert when in close proximity to the donkey.

Sport's lack of attention was the weakness that caused the kick in the head. I knew he failed to pay enough attention. While dogs can be trained to respond to a lot of commands there is not anyway that I know to train a dog to be attentive, or watchful.

This whole incident makes me think of the current state of the American church, or Christians in America. Now that we have witnessed the reality of physical danger from terrorists who would like to destroy us, perhaps we can rest in the shade long enough to get our senses and then spend some time in the kennel recovering and planning. At that juncture perhaps we can go back out as His under-shepherds and function with more watchfulness, more wisdom, and more understanding that we are in the midst of a spiritual war.

"For the Lord gives wisdom, and from his mouth come knowledge and understanding. He holds victory in store for the upright, he is a shield to those whose walk is blameless, for he guards the course of the just and protects the way of his faithful ones". (Proverbs 2:6-8)

39

Following an Empty Bucket

Sons are a heritage from the Lord, children a reward from him. (Psalm 127:3)

October 2002. One day in late January I carried a five-gallon bucket of shelled corn into a pasture where some of my sheep were eating hay that I had put out earlier in the day. I called to them and then began pouring the grain out in small piles of approximately two pounds per pile. The intent was to pour the grain out in such a manner that there would be plenty of room for all the ewes to eat.

Anyone who has experience working with sheep understands that one must pour out grain quickly, and then in the same manner get out of the way of the sheep or they will push and shove making it difficult for you to stand or even walk away. On that particular day I actually poured out most of the grain before calling the ewes, and then quickly moved out of the area. When I was about 200 feet away from the piles of corn I turned to see if all of the sheep were eating grain. I was not too surprised to see that some of the ewes were following me. Well, it would be accurate to say they were following an empty bucket. You see, without the bucket, they would not follow me in such a circumstance.

Following an empty bucket is one thing; to walk past several piles of corn to get to the empty bucket is another. Within seconds of the moment I turned and saw the ewes following I was reminded of one certainty. God has poured out his blessings upon the United States of America. However, one blessing in particular became extremely vivid in my mind that day in the sheep pasture; God has blessed us with our children.

The Bible says, "Sons are a heritage from the Lord, children a reward from him." (Psalm 127:3) Just like a flash of lightening, God showed me that even though he has poured out his blessing upon us by the children given to us, we have failed to fully understand and appreciate such a blessing. I don't need to enumerate the ways in which parents in America passed by their children in order to follow a multitude of empty buckets.

Identifying problems is relatively simple, while working toward solutions can be a greater challenge. However, in the case of our children, including those still in the womb, let us begin with an intense focus on the fact that sons (and daughters) are a heritage from the Lord. Let's not pass them by in pursuit of some empty bucket.

40

Taming the Coyotes

Be self-controlled and alert. Your enemy the devil prowls around like a roaring lion looking for someone to devour.
(1 Peter 5:8)

October 2002. The coyote is a very serious enemy of my sheep flock. I use several specific management practices to protect my flock, but I have never tried to tame the coyotes so they would not devour my sheep. I know, taming coyotes sounds a bit stupid. As long as we are on the topic of stupid ideas let's consider some others. Specifically I wish to point out some in the political/social/spiritual realms.

The very week of this writing we learned that North Korean leaders have admitted that they are developing a nuclear weapons program. Several years ago the Clinton administration, with the volunteer help of former president Jimmy Carter, entered into an agreement with North Korean leaders that we would help them (to the tune of hundreds of millions of dollars) develop nuclear energy for domestic use so long as they would promise that they would not develop nuclear weapons with the technology and the money we would provide them. We were basically offering them a bribe.

Agreements made between honorable people are acceptable, while any agreement between a wicked communist regime and America is foolish on our part. Of course history has shown that Bill Clinton himself was a very dishonorable president and Jimmy Carter a very weak and naive president. At any rate, since America has had threats from several different enemies, it is imperative that our leaders be self-controlled and alert, just as the Bible says. While President George W. Bush seems to be the right man for a time such as this, there are many liberal leftists who are either down right anti-American or naive enough to think you can talk the enemy into a peace settlement, or tame a coyote, so to speak.

Efforts to protect my sheep flock include controlling the sheep and/or controlling the environment for them. For example, some animals are kept inside a barn during the night hours to provide protection. Some animals are allowed to graze in pastures surrounded by woodland, while more vulnerable sheep are not put in those areas. We also have two Great Pyrenees guard dogs that stay near the sheep to protect the flock from predatory animals.

All the measures we take to protect the flock are based upon our knowledge of sheep and our knowledge of the coyote as a predator. For example, coyotes prefer to hunt during the night hours. They are also more intense hunters in the month of May when females are nursing pups. I also classify my sheep into three groups as to their vulnerability. In summary, there are several factors we consider as we set in place procedures to protect our flock. Of paramount importance is that we understand our sheep and that we understand the enemy.

Consider now some social/spiritual implications for this "Taming the Coyotes" piece. I have stated many times during the course of at least 10 years that educating our children is too important to ignore the dangers of sending them daily to government schools. I know of nothing that is more like an attempt to tame the coyotes than all the efforts Christians make to change government schools. We need to wise up; we will not change the basic government school mentality any quicker than I would be able to tame the coyotes roaming on and near my property.

For example, Christians often become elected to school boards thinking they will have an impact. Sure they can be a positive factor, but the possible gains are minuscule in relation to the overall scheme of things. Gains made in a single local school district is a little like taming one coyote only to discover you did not change the nature of *Canis latrans*. Furthermore, the forests and prairies are loaded with untamed coyotes that out number any that might be made docile. I think we also tend to think that things are okay if our children go to a half decent government school. We need to keep a broader perspective. If your school is perfect, it doesn't change the fact that the majority of schools are in a free fall toward mediocrity, immorality and general dumbing down of our children. We need to keep some national perspective, as none of us are isolationists. (Plus isolation is not biblical.)

In our situation the coyote was not even found in this geographic area 20 years ago. Now it is impossible for one farmer to control them, but he can learn to change sheep management. The truth is we need to change the environment for our children just as I did with my sheep. We must provide them with a shepherding environment, as opposed to one where it is obvious that many influences are aimed at devouring our innocent lambs. The family, not a government school, is the proper shepherding environment for our children.

41

Paths of Righteousness for His Name's Sake

– He guides me in paths of righteousness for his name's sake. (Psalm 23:3)

Spring 2003. A few days ago I left the house early in the morning to discover that more than one hundred of my sheep were in my neighbor's pasture. I can recall at least four instances within the past two weeks that one or more of my sheep were "outa pocket." I often use the expression out-of-pocket, which means sheep are in some place other than where they should be. So long as they are outa pocket but still on my land then the problem is not so serious as being over in the neighbor's field.

Most livestock producers live by a code of ethics that says things can get serious when your livestock gets through the fence on to a neighbor's property. The issue is not necessarily damage from the livestock. In fact, my neighbor was gone and was not to return until several days after that morning I found my sheep in his pasture. I could have left them there several days, but the first thing I did after that discovery was to get Sport, our Border Collie herding dog and move the sheep back to where they belonged. The issue among honorable livestock producers is their name. We do not want our name associated with a bunch of sheep that are out of control and will never stay where they belong. Most every time a neighbor's livestock has gotten into my fields the owner has been very apologetic and usually offers some payment for any damages. These men want to do what is right and do not want to be known as that farmer who can't keep his animals under control.

The prophet Isaiah said, "We all, like sheep, have gone astray." (Isaiah 53:6) I think most Christians understand what that means, but when David wrote the line that says "he guides me in paths of righteousness for His name's sake," a somewhat different twist is revealed. Do we realize that Christians who go on wrong paths, go the wrong direction, and generally go the way of the world, that the namesake of our Holy God is damaged?

One of the common criticisms of Christians is that we don't act any different than the world. Many who reject Christianity do so because they do not perceive Christians to be any different. This, of course, is not a new revelation I have; most of us understand the problem. However I do wish to point out some serious problems, as we look at large groups of people who call themselves Christians.

- Recent polls have shown that the divorce rate among Christians is slightly higher than the rest of the population.
- Among the many Baby Boomers who claim to be born again, one-third believes Jesus is not the only way to heaven.
- About one-third of these born again Boomers believe in reincarnation.

The elite leaders of several denominations continue to raise issues such as abortion rights and the rights of homosexuals to fill the pulpit as pastor or priest. These should be non issues in Christianity; God has already settled those issues. Ask any knowledgeable minister and he will admit that a large number of seminaries are not of God. Many false teachers, who claim to be Christians, are making it difficult for the faithful remnant to get the truth to the masses. These people damage His name because they fail to walk in paths of righteousness.

Most praying Christians likely pray for our nation's leaders. For me personally, I am also praying that God will remove the wolves in sheep's clothing. If leaders do not accept the righteousness of God, then we don't need them leading others astray.

For my name's sake I want my sheep to stay in my pasture. That is why I quickly return them when they stray. In addition to damaging my name they set up circumstances where sheep on wrong paths will eventually bring destruction to themselves. The sheep simply don't understand their destructive ways like I do.

In a like manner we Christians don't understand how some paths can lead to our destruction. That's why the Bible is so crucial for the renewing of our minds. We need to seek God like never before and soundly reject those doctrines that are contrary to the Word of God. We need to let Him examine our heart to reveal any of the more subtle ways we are going astray and ask that Him to lead us in paths of righteousness for His name's sake.

42

Culling the Greenheads

That kind of persuasion does not come from the one who calls you. 'A little yeast works through the whole batch of dough.' I am confident in the Lord that you will take no other view. The one who is throwing you into confusion will pay the penalty, whoever he may be. (Galatians 5:8-10)

Summer 2004. Two days ago I took three greenheads to market. They were young adult sheep in their prime, but they had to go. I will not tolerate rogue sheep and risk having the entire flock lead astray.

Each spring as the grass gets greener on the other side of the fence we tend to have more problems with sheep going through the strands of electric fence into adjoining pastures. Once an animal learns it can burst through the electric fence it can do so at will, without pain. Our close observation of the flock can minimize the problem. For example, if sheep seem too tempted to go through a pasture fence we sometimes merely move them to a different pasture.

This spring was different. We had three ewes that were constantly in the wrong pasture. I finally isolated them one day and painted their heads green with a special paint for marking on wool. I kept them from the flock and inside a barn for about a week. I had no problems with sheep leaving the pasture that week. I then returned the three "greenheads" to the pasture – sure enough sheep were going through fences again, and guess what color they had on their heads. That's right – GREEN. So we had properly identified all the rogue sheep.

Since they were near the end of pregnancy I did not wish to sell them at that time. Therefore I tried various management practices to reform the greenheads hoping they would not lead others into the same bad habits. We had them on the farm for several weeks giving their newborn lambs time enough to grow before we weaned them and sold their mothers. It was a struggle because we could not reform the greenheads, and it was not practical to keep them in the barn all the time. I'm sure you have some understanding of my dilemma during that period.

What about the church? Who are the greenheads? The worst ones are not in the congregation. The worst ones are the civil leaders, the politicians, the public school systems, and any in our culture that go the wrong way. The Bible says, as shown in our key Scripture verse, that "A little yeast works through the whole batch of dough." I had to sell three sheep that otherwise were prime looking animals at a nice productive age. I really hated to remove them from the flock; it was a hard decision in one way, but easy in another. It was hard because they were productive, but it was also easy, knowing I was separating my flock from three rogue sheep.

Christians need to begin making some hard decisions. When will we take inventory of all the rogue influences, especially those who adversely affect our children? When will we decide that public schools, for example, are leading our young lambs into places away from The Good Shepherd? Why let the greenheads lead our children astray? There are too many Christians who lack the wisdom to distinguish between those who can be reformed and those who (or what) cannot (e.g., green-headed public school systems). And by the way, if I had sheltered my lambs in the barn (church) on Sunday to protect them from the rogue influences, and then put them back in the pasture Monday through Saturday, you know as well as I do that the Sunday management would not have negated the behavior of the greenheads the rest of the week. If you are a pastor you should realize that you have some responsibility about where the children of your congregation are grazing Monday through Saturday. Isolating the lambs in your barn on Sunday is not good enough. If we don't take drastic action soon then God may paint our heads green.

43

My Sheep

I am the good shepherd; I know my sheep and my sheep know me– (John 10:14)

Fall 2004. I'm no theologian, but I do know a few things about the behavior of sheep. Since the Bible uses so many references to sheep, I am fortunate to be able to observe my flock of more than 200 sheep and spend time studying Scripture to look for new insight in God's eternal Word. Jesus made the statement, "I know my sheep and my sheep know me – " (John 10:14) What does God mean by "my sheep know me"? I suppose many Christians would readily say that those who have accepted Jesus as their personal Savior would be the ones who belong to Him. The wording of the verse implies that there are other sheep that do not belong to Jesus. Later in the same chapter of the book of John, Jesus tells some Jews, "– you do not believe because you are not my sheep. My sheep listen to my voice; I know them, and they follow me." (John 10:26-27)

Unlike other farm animal species, sheep depend very heavily upon the care by man, yet they are the least likely to become docile. In other words sheep are very dependent upon the shepherd, but are reluctant to get close to the shepherd. For example, in an open pasture I probably cannot get within 10 feet of any sheep under normal circumstances. With a sheep-herding dog near, the sheep will allow me to get closer, because they fear the dog. They still tend to move away if I attempt to touch one of them. If I spent more time with them then that behavior would likely change.

This behavior of my sheep reminds me of what I have seen among church-goers. Some are there because they desire to be part of a group. They may want to get reasonably close to Jesus, but not close enough to get the touch of the Master. They know there seems to be some safety, some sanctuary in being part of a church group, but they just never surrender all in order to become one of His sheep. They know some things about Jesus, but they do not KNOW Jesus.

I am basically saying that my sheep do not know me as well as Jesus' sheep know Him. Most of the time my sheep know me well enough to know who I am, but not well enough to follow me. Only under unusual circumstances will they follow me. Jesus made it clear that His sheep follow him. It's rather discouraging to know that research has shown that only about 50 percent of the pastors in America believe that the Bible is the inspired Word of God. My question to those false shepherds is this, "What is your point in pretending to be a minister of the Good News if you don't believe the Bible is the Good News?" Do you trust your intellect, or that of another man to be superior to the Bible? These guys apparently trust their own intellect to be superior to anything God has to offer. I pity the rest of the flock when the so-called shepherd is lost. In other words, how can a congregation know the voice of the Good Shepherd if the person leading them does not know His voice?

There is one more verse in that 10th chapter of John that is very important. After Jesus said, "My sheep listen to my voice; I know them, and they follow me." (vs. 27) He said. "I give them eternal life, and they shall never perish; no one can snatch them out of my hand." (vs. 28) What could be more important than eternal life and to never perish? It's the difference between knowing something about a man named Jesus and having a personal relationship with the Son of God, so close that He knows you, you know His voice, and you follow Him.

44

Good Dogs and Other Dogs

Blessed is the man who does not walk in the counsel of the wicked or stand in the way of sinners or sit in the seat of mockers– (Psalm 1:1)

March 7, 2005. I think all Bible believing churches should invite a local public school principal to preach in their church. Perhaps this should be done as much as three Sundays each month. A pattern of rotation among different principals would give variety. It might be a good idea to look for other public school teachers to be put in the rotation as well. Perhaps the public school superintendent could speak once a year.

I will be quick to point out that these people should not be required to be Christians in order to speak in your Sunday morning worship service. I know that idea will rub a lot of people the wrong way, but I am trying to make suggestions that would be fair and consistent. Perhaps the believers in your congregation could be salt and light for the nonbeliever speaking in your pulpit. I have seen many pastors who protect their pulpit with a fierce determination to keep the wrong people from getting in front of "his flock" and giving out wrong information; things that fail to line up with biblical principles. Some men are VERY adamant about keeping such influence from their congregation.

Dogs, dogs everywhere, but all are not the same. I've switched gears now to talk about my sheep flock and my dogs. We have two Border Collie dogs that are extremely valuable at helping me herd the flock, or move them about the barns, the pastures and any place I wish to direct them. These two are kept in the kennel until I am ready to have them work. I have two Great Pyrenees dogs that provide protection for the sheep flock. At least one guard dog runs loose at all times to go where he pleases as he provides protection.

A few days ago I heard one of the guard dogs start to give a distinctive bark, one that warns a potential predator. I knew the bark and I soon saw a problem. Three stray dogs in the valley below me were approaching our farm. Our guard dog was sending a signal, "You stay away lest I come after you." Stray dogs are potential killers. Until we purchased the guard dogs we lost many sheep to coyotes and wild dogs. I like my herding dogs; they serve a valuable function. I like my guard dogs; they too are very valuable. Stray dogs, wild or not, are unwelcome. Like the pastor who guards his flock, I don't want the wrong kind of dogs with my sheep.

So what does all this have to do with inviting public school personnel into your local church to fill the pulpit at least three weeks a month or 75% of the time? It's about poor influences on our children and grandchildren in a place where God is forbidden.

I doubt your pastor would invite a nonbeliever to fill the pulpit to speak to the adults in the church. Does it bother your pastor that five days a week (more than 75% of the children's time) teaching is provided to children in his congregation at public schools that do not acknowledge Jesus Christ and/or God unless it is to blatantly disallow the mention of His name? I would hope this situation bothers your pastor, but I will venture a guess that it would bother him more if you suggest a nonbeliever preach to the congregation.

I trust you realize by now that I was being facetious in suggesting nonbelievers from a public school to speak to your congregation. I do pray that leaders in America's church congregations will pause long enough to realize how absurd it is to be so "religious" about who stands in the pulpit talking to adults, who should have a degree of Christian maturity, about them on the one hand, and yet on the other hand are blinded to the dangers of having our young immature lambs (our children) being taught daily in a system that is flawed by any biblical measure you use. Incidentally, my young lambs are much more susceptible to predators than my adult sheep. A stray dog among my lambs is ALWAYS a greater threat than such a dog in a pasture of adult sheep.

It takes a real leap of faith to believe that the public school systems have anything to offer that is better than what God can provide through Christians who clearly understand God's Word and who are willing to make a commitment to provide solid Christian training via home schooling and/or private Christian schools. It takes a gigantic leap of faith to believe the public school system has a neutral effect upon the moral/spiritual development of our nation's children.

The Barna Research Group has shown that a large majority of Christian teens fail to continue to attend church after leaving home at 18 years of age, implying that the worldview influence of public schools has dominated their thinking. Do we want God's best training for our children? If so, where are the shepherds willing to lead in this direction? If you remain unconvinced, I suggest you read the 34th chapter of Ezekiel.

45

Through the Working Chute

*Jesus answered, I am the way and the truth and the life.
No one comes to the Father except through me.* (John 14:6)

August 30, 2005. Sheep are gregarious; they like to stay together. They have a strong herding, or flocking instinct, as we shepherds describe them. People are that way too. God has described man as being like sheep, so our study of behaviors of this animal can often give us insight as to how God sees us. A study of these animals also shows that each individual sheep must eventually come by the shepherd for treatment. And people?

As a shepherd I really appreciate sheep that flock together. If my sheep are grazing in one of the mountainous areas where they can easily hide among the trees, then it is of considerable benefit to find them all grazing together. Otherwise finding them could be a real hide and seek game. Also the strong flocking instinct helps my herding dogs. When a dog follows my command and goes running to gather the sheep it would be near impossible for him if the sheep scattered in all directions upon seeing the dog. However, once the sheep observe the dog coming, the normal reaction is that the entire flock begins running inward toward the center of their grazing area. This flocking together is like a giant magnet. Once the group is gathered, then a single herding dog can drive a flock of 200 to 300 sheep without much trouble.

Although the strong flocking instinct has its advantages there are times when it is important for every single sheep to come by me in the working chute. Let me first explain the working chute. My chute is 16 feet long with a funnel shaped area where sheep enter the 18-inch wide chute single file. A gate at the opposite end serves to hold the sheep until I finish working with them. A primary treatment I use on each sheep is an oral dose of medicine to kill internal parasites. EVERY sheep must get the treatment to be protected. I must personally minister, as it were, to each and every one. It could be considered the present day "anointing my head with oil" as described in the 23rd Psalm.

Now let's get back to His sheep. Most people like to be part of one or more groups. For example, a person might be reluctant to travel several hundred miles to help some stranger in need, but would enjoy going as a part of a group work team to help others. The peer influence is particularly evident among teens in America. However, being part of a church group does not make one a Christian. You don't become a Christian just because your parents took you to church meetings while you lived with them. You have to go one-on-one with God, and Jesus said it clearly, "I am the way and the truth and the life." No one comes to the father except through me." (John 14:6)

The group dynamics among Christians can be great, but the personal relationship with God comes after we repent of our sins and in faith we accept Jesus Christ as Savior. We then communicate with God through the Holy Spirit. Yes, others can pray with you and for you, but when Jesus died on the cross the temple curtain was split open top to bottom allowing believers to enter the Most Holy Place. Our relationship to Him can come in the quiet times as we listen to His voice, or while we study the Bible to show ourselves approved. This definitely requires individual effort on my part and on your part if we are to have that personal relationship.

Some current trends among Christians are very disturbing. I see two distinct problems.

1. The "I want my way" mentality that says I am seeking a congregation that meets my needs (i.e. seeker friendly)
2. Following after prominent men and ideologies contrary to biblical commands

Jesus is the way, not Billy Graham, Joel Osteen or Rick Warren just to name three prominent Christian leaders. Billy Graham has preached to more people than any other man in history. Joel Osteen pastors the largest congregation in America and Rick Warren is the poster boy for filling the church pews with his Purpose Driven (PD) doctrine.

Just one quick point about the PD frenzy among Christians in America right now; Jesus died on the cross for our sins and there is clearly one Book, the Bible, that has all the keys. Do not let other books be your guide.

Graham and Osteen both recently missed golden opportunities to say the right things while being interviewed on a secular TV show, Larry King Live. When King asked pointed questions to each of these men in separate interviews about whether or not Christians are the only ones going to heaven or not, they both failed the test. They both hedged. They both said they couldn't say that Christians are the only ones who go to heaven. They missed the opportunity to simply quote the Bible. How difficult is that for seasoned Christians? Why not just quote the Bible? How about, Jesus said, "I am the way, the truth, and the life. No one comes to the Father except through me."

Jesus Christ is either who He says He is, or He is a big liar. Take your pick. If you think He is a liar, say so. If you think He is the way to God the Father, then say so. Don't squirm in your seat and tell the lost in this world that you don't know!

46

A Concluding Track

Will You Choose Pasture or Barn Lambing?

Go into all the world and preach the good news to all creation. (Mark 16:15)

October 21, 2005. I am in the final stages of finishing the details of getting these writings to fit the proper mold for publication. I am literally at the stage of trying to get the manuscript in proper form, the grammar errors reduced, the correct punctuation, etc. A serious problem has visited my flock of sheep that prompts this concluding S*heep Track.*

One of our Great Pyrenees guard dogs, Bo, was found dead yesterday. He was in his prime, a relatively young dog. He is the large white dog shown in the sheep/snow scene photo in one of the early pages of this book. Since these guard dogs are allowed to roam free in order to be effective watchdogs for our flock, it is virtually impossible to protect them from many hazards they face. Just last week someone shot a guard dog that belonged to a farm family 10 miles from here. Did my dog die of natural causes? Probably not. Did he ingest something that was poisonous? Perhaps; we just don't know what caused his death.

How serious is this death of our dog? In a worst case scenario, with no guard dog, we could expect to loose half our lamb crop next spring because they are scheduled to be born out in open pasture fields. Coyotes will devour newborn lambs like someone picking cherries. Things are already set in motion; we can't just purchase a trained dog that is mature enough to guard the flock. They must be raised with the flock from the time they are weaned pups. That's the worst case scenario should something happen to our other dog, Peep.

Biblically, things are already set in motion. A lot of people like to spend time talking about the Last Days. The frequent hurricanes hitting land in America is just one example of what motivates people to discuss the Last Days. Even as I write this, hurricane Wilma is scheduled to hit Florida in a few days. Frankly, on an individual basis, every day is a last day because no one has a guarantee about tomorrow. We need to be concerned for all lost souls every day.

The whole issue with my flock centers on the fact that we have our lambs born in pastures rather than in a barn. Why? Knowledgeable animal scientist say barns are usually built for the comfort of the shepherd rather than the welfare of the entire flock of sheep. Lambs born and raised in a barn usually do have a better chance of survival, but the labor is intense, and the size of the barn sets the limits on size of the flock.

What about the church? Are we birthing in church buildings or out in the "pastures" where people live? I know a church congregation that has three church buildings lining a city block. Each was constructed as a sanctuary for worship services. They are small, medium, and large, reflecting the growth of that congregation. Now the congregation appears to be over its head in debt trying to pay for the largest one because so few people occupy the pews each Sunday. That compares to a sheepherder who chooses to lamb indoors and builds more barns and bigger barns that ultimately put him in debt.

Here is another important point. The guard dogs are necessary for the potential new sheep (newborn lambs), not for the adult sheep. In other words, if I just want to maintain an adult flock, then coyotes are an insignificant threat. Do church services that focus on nurture of the adult sheep in comfortable pews seem a little like a barn lambing situation?

Jesus did not say, "Bring the lost into a building so they can become 'born again.'" He said, "Go." He said, "—go and make disciples of all nations–." (Matt. 28:19) He said, "Go into all the world and preach the good news–." (Mark 16:15)

Pasture lambing has its risks. It takes special management, but we can birth more lambs, and we don't have the expense of building larger barns.

Are you part of a church congregation? If so, is your emphasis on the many sheep out in the pasture, or is your focus on the comfort of a shepherd and a few pew-sitting sheep in an expensive barn?

About the Author

The author was born April 3, 1941, in the same room where he wrote *Sheep Tracks, Biblical Insights From A Sheepherder.* The book was completed when he was 64 years old. He developed an interest in agriculture as he grew up on the family farm. This led to his study at three universities where he obtained degrees of B.S., M.S., and Ph.D. in the animal sciences. He taught at a university for 11 years before returning to the home farm in 1982 to raise sheep. His head knowledge about sheep was then enhanced with heart knowledge as he spent much time studying the Bible, managing his sheep flock, and seeking God in prayer.

He and his wife Glenda founded Psalm 23 Camp on their farm in 1985 where part of the emphasis is on sheep/shepherd relationships. In 1993 they started Servants At Work (SAW) as an outreach to local people and to missionaries in Central America.

The Rowans have five children and nine grandchildren.

Sheep Tracks Online

This book has focused on Dennis Rowan's insights as a sheepherder based upon work with his sheep and other farm related experiences. Some of the chapters here have been posted at www.psalm23camp.com during the past three years in a column titled *Sheep Tracks*.

All of Rowan's observations in life do not come directly from watching four-legged sheep. While watching the behaviors of people he has written about some of these actions that don't necessarily have a connection with what he has seen in his sheep flock. In other words, as people and events pass by, he may see a biblical connection and then write an article that has been posted in a column called *Through The working Chute*. These too, are found at the above web address.

Most of his online writing in the future will be posted at www.HisSheepTracks.com.

Psalm 23 Camp

Dennis and Glenda Rowan started Psalm 23 Camp in July 1985. The camp is located on a farm that has been in the Rowan family for four generations. The first camp provided a three-day camp experience without charge for 14 local children ages eight to eleven. The available resources included a 300 acre farm, some family pack tents, a pickup camper, two picnic tables, two outhouses and some part-time volunteers to help the Rowan's. All meals were cooked over a open campfire and campers helped with fire building, dish washing, and other duties.

The camp has undergone much change during the past 20 years. A dairy barn built in the 1940's and 50's has been converted to a unique facility that houses the kitchen and dining area, plus rooms for recreation, meeting and lounging. Campers stay in motel-type rooms. More information can be found at www.psalm23camp.com.

Servants At Work

West Virginia. Whereas Psalm 23 Camp was established in 1985 to provide children with something to do, the Servants-At-Work (S.A.W.) camps were started in 1993 as a way of involving young people in doing something for other people. A major objective is to provide a balance of service, spiritual growth, and recreation for the campers.

The S.A.W. camps involve teens in projects in and near Monroe County, West Virginia that assist the elderly, disabled and other needy families with home construction projects. Minor home repair and painting are common types of work projects to help families. More complex projects, including help with new home construction, are usually available each summer.

Foreign Missions. S.A.W. trips to assist missionaries in Central America are also a part of this ministry.

Printed in the United States
56357LVS00002B/463-510